Autograph

COLLECTING

SECRETS

Tools and Tactics
FOR THROUGH-THE-MAIL, IN-PERSON
AND CONVENTION SUCCESS

TROY A RUTTER
Foreword by Jack Smalling

Astralight Media
10153 1/2 Riverside Dr. #436
Toluca Lake, CA 91602

Library of Congress Cataloging-In-Publication Data
Rutter, Troy A
    Autograph collecting secrets : Tools and tactics for through-the-mail, in-person and convention success / Troy A. Rutter
    ISBN: 9780982638835
    LCCN: 2016915198
    1. collecting-hobbies-United States 2. celebrities

First Edition: November 2016
Printed in the United States of America

10 9 8 7 6 5 4 3 2 1

CONTENTS

FOREWORD

The basics of collecting sports autographs haven't changed much since I first started back in 1962. Two main options prevail: meeting a player either at a game, hotel, or in the wild, or sending a letter through the mail. With over 100,000 autographs and 20 books, it is continually rewarding to help both new and seasoned collectors enjoy the hobby. With positive sales of my latest book, *The Autograph Collector's Handbook #18*, it is easy to put to rest claims of the hobby going away anytime soon. Fans living far away from team stadiums still enjoy connecting with their favorite athletes through the mail - and will for years to come.

In this book, Troy Rutter takes both novice and experienced autograph collectors through many tips and tricks of obtaining sports and entertainment autographs. The hobby landscape has changed from even just 10 years ago, and Troy's experience in Internet sleuthing as well as being a leader in the online autograph community is exemplary. Outsiders may think it is as simple as just "sending a letter," but Troy's advice on crafting the perfect letter-of-request and strategies for pitcher and catcher reporting, pre-season, regular season, and post-season autograph hunting is spot on.

There must be something in the water in Ames, Iowa that has lead both myself and Troy to this rewarding hobby. But whether you live in Ames, Los Angeles, Miami or Sydney Australia, you can acquire a great autograph collection - all from the comfort of your own home.

Good luck!

Jack Smalling
September, 2016

INTRODUCTION

If you are picking up this book and perusing the contents and the introduction, you may already be interested in one of the most exciting hobbies in the world: autograph collecting! You are definitely in the right place to find out more about the hobby.

Autograph collecting can take many forms. Hobbyists collect all kinds of autographs: historical memorabilia of presidents, serial killers, poets, playwrights, and the tried-and true athletes and entertainment celebrities. If a signature fits on an item, someone probably collects it. Over the years I have seen spoons signed by Paula Deen and red staplers signed by Stephen Root of the film *Office Space*. I've seen all sorts of signed knick-knacks, toys, games, photos, baseball bats, cards, mannequins, napkins … everything!

What draws people to the hobby is obtaining a certain autograph, of a certain person, in a certain place in history. People who collect autographs in person do so as a memento of meeting someone famous. Those who collect through the mail (TTM) do it for the thrill of sending something away to their favorite celebrity, never knowing if it will come back or not… and joy if it does.

More than anything, we do it because it is fun. And, thanks to the Internet, we can share our successes with others who enjoy collecting as well. Online communities have sprung up around the hobby, bringing all of us closer together and uniting us in our endless search for our most wanted signatures.

I wish I had this book when I started collecting autographs through the mail in a small town in Iowa. In the following pages, you will get tips and tricks for increasing your success rate when requesting an autograph from your favorite celebrity. By using the tools in this book, you should see your mailbox fill up and your collection grow larger.

There are a lot of scams and fake autographs out there. While I can't be there beside you while you search online auction sites or the collector's store down the street, this book will help you learn the warning signs of fake autographs and offer legitimate ways to buy items for your collection.

There are two major categories of autograph collectors this book is *not* for. This book is not for the historical collector who wants to collect as many Abraham Lincoln signatures as they can. This book is also not for the high-end collector who wants a signed guitar by all of the Beatles. While those are both great niches, in this book I focus on current celebrities who can be contacted in-person or through-the-mail.

I want to thank all of the TTMers who have made the community something to be proud of. I can't mention everyone, but I really want to thank Stacy Shaffer and Zane Savage for welcoming me into the Autograph Weekly Podcast crew. Even though there were some (very) late nights and recording mis-haps and drama - it holds a special place in my journey.

Thanks-you also to my two editors for this book: Jim Arrowood and David Wharton. Your advice and proofing were invaluable.

It is a wonderful time to be an autograph collector! Please join me at any of my social media profiles, or my website, and let me tag along with you on your journey.

Here's hoping every day is a giant mail day!

Troy Rutter
September, 2016

GLOSSARY

Any job or hobby has its own terminology, and autograph collecting is no different. Newcomers to the hobby often struggle to learn all the vocabulary and how it relates to what they are collecting. After all, we just want to mail something out, have someone sign it, and have it mailed it, back, right?

Below is a list of the most common abbreviations you will find in autograph collecting, located conveniently at the beginning of the book instead of the end. New additions to this list can be found on my website at *ttmautograph.com.* If you encounter a new term, head over to my web site and see if it is there. If not, go ahead and email me and I will get right on it so the reference guide is complete and helpful to other collectors.

4x6, 8x10, 11x17: Various photo sizes. These are noted without the inches indicator.

ANK: Attempted Not Known. An acronym on a returned piece of mail meaning there is something wrong with the address.

AP: Autopen. A mechanical device that uses a writing instrument to sign photos in bulk.

B/W: Black and White.

Blaster Box: A trading card box containing a set number of cards.

Box Break: An opening of a box of cards by collectors who pay to be included, oftentimes selecting the cards they want to receive by team and/or player.

CAC: Contact Any Celebrity. A subscription website containing celebrity addresses.

Channel: A "homepage" for a creator on YouTube.

CISP: Color Inscribed Signed Photo. A color photo that is signed and personalized to someone.

COA: Certificate of Authenticity. A document declaring the supposed authenticity of a photo.

CSP: A Color Signed Photo, usually not inscribed or personalized.

Cut: A signature cut from a document and placed onto a card or matte for display.

FOE: Forwarding Order Expired. A Return to Sender (RTS) received from an address where mail used to be forwarded, but is no longer.

HOF: Hall of Fame. Any of the Hall of Fame organizations for various sports. Also used to denote inductees to the organizations.

Favorite: Same as a "Like" on Facebook.

Folback: Slang for "follow back." Used when someone follows or subscribes to your social media account and wants you to do the same in reciprocity.

Follow: To "Subscribe" to a person's social media feed.

FS/FT: For sale or for trade

Grade: A number value given to a card based on its condition.

Gravity Feeder: An open box of retail card packs on display that feeds more cards to the open area of the box when packs below are removed.

GU: Game used.

Hit: An autograph, patch card, numbered card, or any relic randomly inserted into a retail pack of cards.

Hobby Box: A sealed box of trading cards containing a set number of packs. Contains at least a predetermined number and type of hits.

Hot Pack: A retail pack of cards that searchers have identified as having a "hit" or relic. Often found by pack searching.

IC: Index Card. A lined or blank heavyweight piece of paper.

IP: In Person. Obtaining an autograph by meeting the person signing.

IRC: International Reply Coupon. A form of postage used to mail items back from foreign countries.

Jumbo Pack: A type of retail pack containing more cards than a normal pack and usually without relics or autograph hits.

ISP: Inscribed Signed Photo. A more generic term for a CISP that can be for either color or black-and-white inscribed photos.

Like: A social media term denoting appreciation for what someone posts.

LOR: Letter of Request. A typed or hand-written request for an autograph.

Mag Case: A heavy-duty protector for cards and other memorabilia that encases the autograph and fastens using a magnet.

MTFB: Mike the Fanboy. A website for celebrity news and autograph addresses.

Page: A type of gathering place on Facebook to post photos, videos, and updates.

PC: Personal Collection. A particular category of a collection revolving around a specific sports figure, team, or TV series.

Penny Sleeve: A thin, clear plastic envelope for cards, designed to protect them from dust, scratches, and fingerprints.

PP: Preprint. An autograph that is actually part of the photograph and not signed.

PSA/DNA: A company who authenticates and grades the quality of a piece of memorabilia or autograph.

PSP: Personalized Signed Photo. An older term for an ISP/CISP.

Pull: Getting a good card, usually an autograph, relic, or numbered card, from a standard card pack. Also called a "hit."

PWE: A plain white envelope, usually business size #10.

Q&A: A popular type of video on YouTube where a collector answers questions from other collectors or subscribers. Also a form of celebrity interview in front of an audience.

Rack Pack: A type of retail pack usually consisting of two sections of cards with a built-in eye for hanging on a display rack. Usually does not contain major hits.

Razz: A form of a box break where people pay for the chance to participate for a lower cost than a typical box break. An example would be a high-end card razz selling 100 spots, and then a random group of 30 will actually be in the break.

Reblog: A feature on Tumblr that reposts a particular post onto your own Tumblr page, giving a link to the original author. Similar to a share on Facebook.

Relic: A general term for a hit in a pack of cards. Covers bat cards, patch cards, game-worn jerseys, and more.

RTS: Return to Sender. A return of your item by the post office without it being signed. This could be due to a variety of reasons, usually specified on a yellow label on the envelope.

SASE: Self-Addressed Stamped Envelope. An envelope including enough postage to mail back to you, pre-filled out so your address is on the "To" line.

Secretarial: A suspected fake autograph, usually signed by a celebrity's secretary, agent, or family member.

Send: A slang term for an entire TTM package: Item, Letter of Request, SASE, and sending envelope.

SCF: Sports Card Forum. An online community for sports card collectors.

SIC: Signed index card.

Slabbed: A graded or authenticated card encased by a third party authenticator such as PSA/DNA or JSA.

ST: Star Tiger. One of the oldest subscription services for tracking your requests and obtaining addresses. Formerly known as Star Archive.

Sub: Subscribe or Subscriber. Mainly used on YouTube or any other website with a feed available, notifying the subscriber of new content.

SWE: Standard White Envelope - usually a #10 or business-size envelope. Also called a Plain White Envelope (PWE).

Thumbnail: A smaller version of an image, or a static image representing a video.

Top Loader: A heavier gauge plastic protector for cards and photos.

Top Ten: A list used by many collectors of their "10 Most Wanted" autographs.

TTM: Through the Mail. A general term for sending a photograph or piece of memorabilia through the mail to a celebrity in hopes of It being returned signed and in good condition.

UACC: Universal Autograph Collector's Club.

VV: Via Venue. Sending an item to a non-permanent location such as a filming address, theatre, or public appearance venue.

CHAPTER 1
MY AUTOGRAPH STORY

Collecting autographs has been a hobby of mine for almost 30 years. I would walk to the post office to buy a small booklet of their gummy little pieces of paper (stamps weren't self-adhesive in the late '80s…) and then spend hours at the library researching where to send my next letter of request. Even before then, I had the players on the Iowa State University basketball team sign my game program. Things have changed since those early days, and through these many years of experience I have become not only a more seasoned collector, but a more realistic one. I know in my heart not every TTM request I send is going to come back and I'm ok with that.

This book is focused on helping beginning to experienced collectors acquire autographs through the mail. I cover aspects of obtaining in-person (IP) signatures and offer convention autograph strategies as well. The autographs I collect center around entertainment and sports personalities, so those are the main genres I will cover. There are many other books detailing how to collect historical autographs of presidents, poets, humanitarians, serial killers, etc. While some of these techniques cross over, the specific niches we will be looking at are entertainment and sports personalities: movies, TV, baseball, football, hockey, mixed martial arts, and more. This category of sports and entertainment autographs covers a wide spectrum of sub-genres as well.

The first autograph I ever obtained was of Iowa State Cyclone star Barry Stevens. Growing up, my family was Barry's "Home Away From Home" family. This was the name for a local family the college athlete could feel a part of, have meals with, etc. Each game would feature one of the players on a giant poster on the reverse side of the score-keeping tally sheet. I kept all of the posters and was able to convince Barry to let me into the locker room to get them signed. Sadly, none of these posters survived.

I didn't really think of autographs again until the eighth grade, when a traveling promotion for *Doctor Who* came to town. There, I met the Fifth Doctor's companion, Janet Fielding. The local PBS station brought in a trailer complete with a mock-up of the inside of the TARDIS, the companion K9 and other original and replica props. One of the main draws to the event was that Fielding would be leading a Question and Answer, Q&A, session after everybody had a chance to tour the semi trailer display.

After the Q&A session, she signed a very poorly printed black-and-white photograph for me. This was promptly framed and hung proudly on my wall. Little did I know of the effect direct sunlight has on a photograph over the years! It has since faded a little, and the whites are more of a cream color.

Janet Fielding, my "first" autograph. (Troy Rutter)

We didn't get many celebrities through my small town, save for a small *Star Trek* convention or two. While I did attend one in which James Doohan appeared, for reasons I don't remember, I did not get an autograph that day.

My first TTM autograph came when I was a sophomore or junior in high school. I was always fascinated by films and wanted to become a filmmaker or actor myself, so I used a computer system called Lexis Nexis to learn which actors were born in my home state of Iowa. The first I found was John Wayne, but he was out of the running for an autograph since he had died several years prior. The next was a young actor, about eight years younger than me, whom I had seen in several films already - Elijah Wood. Using the Lexis Nexis computer system, I was able to find that he was represented by an agency called William Morris, and also by a personal management company run by a man called Brian Swardstrom.

I sent a letter with a return envelope to Mr. Swardstrom, and several months later I received a personalized signed photo of Elijah Wood.

Elijah Wood, my first TTM Autograph (Troy Rutter)

I was hooked.

I would go on to send other requests to a wide variety of celebrities... with little-to-no success since I was relying on their generosity to provide a photo rather than sending one myself. Once in awhile, an envelope would appear and I would try and figure out how long it took, but I never bothered to keep track of the exact dates. I keep track of my requests rather religiously now!

In 1995, after accumulating quite a few autographs and lining the top of my walls with a border of signed photos, I had the chance to take a position with Warner Bros. Studios in California. While there, I also represented many young performers, designing websites and helping them form their "official fan clubs" and internet presence. I took a break from requesting autographs, since I never knew who I might work with someday. In 2001, I returned to Iowa, and while I would send out a request here and there, it really wasn't until 2012 that I decided to get back into autograph collecting.

My life changed.

I learned several people just like me loved collecting autographs. And, just like me, they loved online video. These crazy guys, Zane Savage and Stacy Shaffer, created videos on YouTube and shared their "mail days" with thousands of people through their YouTube channels. After being introduced through YouTube, I found they also recorded a podcast - something I had also done, but abandoned for lack of time. After emailing back and forth and posting my own first few YouTube videos, I was invited to be a part of the Autograph Weekly Podcast and their live YouTube shows. Unfortunately, right about the time I started getting involved, Autograph Weekly began to go on several hiatuses, until the plug was finally pulled. Undeterred, most of us kept creating YouTube videos and developed our own styles and followers on YouTube, Facebook, and the Internet.

I took a little hiatus of my own in 2014 and then came back with a vengeance in mid 2015, after I moved back to Los Angeles once again to work for a major studio. I have seen my YouTube channel and autograph collection grow and have learned a lot from 30 years of autograph collecting. I can't wait to share it with you.

CHAPTER 2

IS AUTOGRAPH COLLECTING DEAD?

There have been many articles written over the past year or so proclaiming that autograph collecting is dead, and that the selfie (an informal photograph of a celebrity and one or more other people) is the new autograph.

Not so.

The death of autograph collecting is as much a hoax as the reported deaths of many celebrities before their time. Before selfies "killed" autograph collecting, people claimed the "digital autograph" would spell the end of the hobby.

Neither has been the case.

Attending a convention such as San Diego Comic-Con, or even some of the smaller conventions, the longest lines in the entire complex (other than the pre-registration badge pick-up lines) are at the autograph tables. Fans wait in a queue for hours just to get an autographed photo from

A signed selfie with "Mike Teevee" from *Willy Wonka* using an iOS app (Troy Rutter)

a celebrity - often at a very steep price. Selfies with a celebrity are often $10-$20 extra, if they are allowed at all. Celebrities who have just one role on a popular science fiction TV show or movie often appear at these conventions, charging for their signature, as do retired wrestlers, comedians, YouTube creators, and even professional cosplayers (people who dress up as movie, film, or anime characters). Some celebrities, such as Mark Hamill and William Shatner, are known to charge over $150 for a single autographed photo - and people gladly pay it for the chance to meet their heroes.

As the world of entertainment changes, so do the various genres of autograph collecting. Collecting autographs of political figures gave way to radio, TV, and movie stars. Baseball, football, and other sports figures have always been popular. In today's autograph world, there are also new genres of celebrities from YouTube, Vine, and Musical.ly, as well as professional cosplayers. There are an infinite number of different niches and audiences. You may think you are the only one who collects autographed books of mid-grade novel authors starting with the letter Q

... but, chances are, there is another collector out there somewhere who does the same thing.

Mark Hamill Autograph obtained in 1994 for $20. He now charges close to $200 (Troy Rutter)

Things changed in the autograph world in 2016, especially when it comes to in-person autographs. Fans were shocked when *The Voice* star Christina Grimmie was killed signing autographs for her fans after a show. Unfortunately, she wasn't the first or only celebrity murdered by a fan: John Lennon, Rebecca Schaeffer, Selena, and others all were taken from us by killers who once claimed to be fans.

In response to Christina Grimmie's murder, the social media convention VidCon used an elaborate labyrinth of corridors to protect its guests from overzealous fans. In addition, several sports teams have announced players will sign for "kids only" after they began to see autograph dealers hound players for two, three, and even ten autographs at a time, which are often promptly listed for sale on online auction sites.

Online auction sites are often cited as a reason many celebrities don't sign autographs at all. But for every celebrity who says they don't sign, there are a hundred or more who do. Even those who say they *don't* may sign under the right circumstances.

Many businesses have sprung up revolving around the world of autograph collecting. Some, like eBay dealers, are oftentimes whispered about and condemned. Others try to be helpful to the autograph community by offering to authenticate and grade signatures. Still others work on behalf of autograph shows, who bring in a few dozen guests at a time and make an event around the people signing - but also sell signed photographs on the side for those who can't attend the actual convention.

Has the world of autograph collecting changed? Absolutely. Like everything, it is constantly changing and evolving.

But the hobby is definitely not dead.

CHAPTER 3

AUTOGRAPH COLLECTING SUPPLIES

Sending a piece of mail and getting it back to you seems like a simple thing, but the more you get into autograph collecting, the more choices you have and the more tools you become aware of. This is true especially when collecting autographs through the mail (TTM). You will hear me say to visit your favorite office supply store a lot in this chapter, but you can also find most of these items at your community's department stores such Target or Walmart, just not in the quantity I recommend buying. Be sure to check out a shopping list at the end of the chapter for your first big TTM shopping spree to get all geared up.

ENVELOPES

The basic item of any TTM request is the envelope, usually the plain white envelope (PWE). Envelopes come in all shapes and sizes, but the ones you will use the most are called a #10. These are the common, white, letter-size envelopes where an 8 ½" x 11" piece of paper can be folded into thirds and placed inside. These envelopes can also hold index cards, 4x6 photos, sports cards, and other small pieces of memorabilia.

Every envelope addressed to a celebrity has its mate: the Self-Addressed Stamped Envelope, or SASE. The SASE is simply another envelope, already stamped and with your return address on it.

For sports cards or 4x6 photos, I actually use two separate sizes of PWE's. A #10 for the envelope I'm sending, and a #6 envelope as the SASE. A #6 envelope is a smaller envelope that fits perfectly inside the #10. See the illustration below.

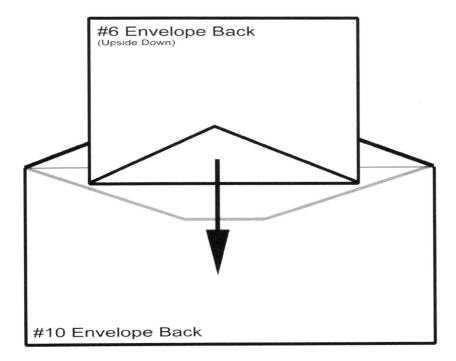

#6 Envelope Back
(Upside Down)

#10 Envelope Back

Obviously, you can't fit an 8x10 photo or a magazine into a standard #10 envelope. For those types of requests, you are going to need some larger sizes. Using the same nesting approach, I like to use 9x12 envelopes as the SASE, and 10x13 envelopes as the mailing envelope for the entire package. You can find these at your favorite office supply store. If you can't find the 10x13 envelopes, you can use another 9x12 envelope and just fold it in half to fit inside the other one.

There are other sized envelopes you can use for photos if you want, ranging from regular thickness to padded, cardboard, or plastic bubbles. My go-to envelopes, however, are always #6 and #10. I usually buy a box of 500 #6 and 500 #10 from an office supply store, and a box of 100 each of 9x12 and 10x13. Those should keep you well stocked for quite some time. If you are starting smaller, you don't have to purchase this many at once. Just buy a box of 50 white envelopes and fold one in half to fit inside the other. I don't like this approach, since your return card may be bent if the envelope is folded, but it is an option.

BUBBLE MAILERS

If you are selling your collection, or want some extra protection, bubble mailers are the way to go. The smallest bubble mailer available in large quantities is 4"x8" #000, and I suggest you buy them in bulk rather than one at a time. You can also try "CD-ROM mailers," which are cardboard without the bubbles, but bubble mailers are pretty much the de facto standard for mailing out multiple cards when selling or trading among collectors. Make sure to use top loaders, penny sleeves, and cardboard to make the package extra rigid.

PAPER

You can find my thoughts on whether to type or handwrite your letters of request in chapter six dealing with TTMs. The paper you use will depend on your choice of handwriting or typing. For typed letters, you can use standard copy paper, or you can choose a heavier brand of "resume" paper to make it stand out a little. For typed letters, I use standard white paper, as opposed to personalized stationery, premium paper, colored paper, or anything else.

For handwritten letters of request, you can use wide or college-ruled lined notebook paper, but I like to use something non-standard, such as a half-sized pad of lined paper. This makes it less obvious when I don't write as much. I have tried using various other colors of paper for hand-written requests, and in my experience it really doesn't matter what size or color of paper - it is a personal preference.

LABELS

If you want to save yourself hours of tedious writing, the use of return address labels is highly recommended. You have probably seen the ads for "rolls" of return address labels with a monogram on them, foil, or other fancy variations. Many companies even promote "Buy one, get one free!" There really isn't a need to spend a lot of money for return address labels. My favorite labels are ones you can just buy at your office supply store, Walmart, or Target.

Return address labels come in many different sizes, but the trick is to get the most for your money. I highly recommend Avery brand 8167 for inkjet printers. These labels are 1/2" x 1 3/4" and work with laser printers as well. There are only 25 sheets for about $14, but that is for 2,000 labels - enough to keep the TTMs coming in for a long time.

Using a computer program such as Microsoft Word, Pages, etc., you can duplicate your return address into a template for the label and print them 30-40 per sheet.

As I explain in chapter six, I use address labels for the return address on the envelope for the send and return, but also as the SASE.

Stamps

US First Class Stamps - Forever Stamps

Ah… the stamp. A small adhesive piece of paper wielding such great power. Whether you are sending autographs from the United States, Canada, Australia, the UK, or anywhere else, it all comes down to the postage stamp. Without it, the chances of getting your beloved autograph back to you are slim to none. (Yes, I said slim - there are stories about collectors receiving their autograph back without a stamp, or the celebrity using one of their own. Be safe, though: stamp responsibly.)

In the United States, the most common stamp used for TTM's, especially sports cards, are Forever Stamps. Once you buy them, you can use them for a first-class letter even if the price of a stamp goes up or down. Stamps come in all different sizes and designs, especially around the holidays. It can be fun to go into the post office and ask what kind of stamps they currently have, and then keep track of the stamps you send during a particular month or season. If you see a snowman stamp come back, even before you open it, you know that was one you sent in a specific time period!

These special Forever Stamps usually come on individual sheets of varying quantities. It is easier to buy them by the sheet rather than individually, and a good rule of thumb is to buy enough so the total number is divisible by two, since you will at least need two for your send and your SASE. So if a sheet has 19 stamps on it, I would by 2 sheets for 28 (enough for 14 TTMs). You don't have to follow this suggestion religiously, as you will always have need for "one more stamp." For instance, if you get at TTM returned as undeliverable, you will have the

SASE from that send available again, so you'll just need one more stamp to send another out.

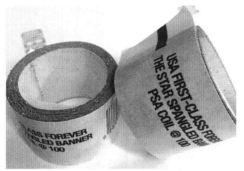

For the hardcore TTM'ers, the post office sells 100-count rolls of stamps featuring a US flag on them. When a sport is in pre-season, I often buy 2-3 rolls to get me ramped up for that particular sport.

I highly recommend buying stamps directly from the post office whenever

200 Forever Stamps, 100 per roll. (Troy Rutter)

possible. For a while, I bought stamps from my bank's ATM, since the post office was always busy. While it is possible to buy them there, there is often a surcharge of up to 20% per stamp. You definitely pay for the convenience.

Post Office Kiosks

Instead of buying stamps from the ATM, I recommend using an automated stamp kiosk located at most US post offices. This is a self-service mecca of TTM goodliness that will come in handy throughout your time collecting autographs. It dispenses special Forever Stamps and can be used to weigh and mail packages without waiting in line. I love the kiosks - when they work! The one in my hometown is routinely out of service when I need to use it, but they are definitely handy.

Since most post office lobbies are open 24 hours, the kiosk is the best place to go when you have a stamp emergency. As I mentioned, avoid the bank ATM at all costs unless the stamp kiosk is out of order. If you use a debit card at the kiosk, the limit appears to be $25 at a time, since I am only ever able to buy 51 stamps per debit card. The stamps that print out are larger than normal stamps and have a code printed on them to let the automatic scanners know they aren't fake.

Standard USPS service kiosk. (Troy Rutter)

"Peanuts" holiday stamps dispensed by a US Post Office kiosk. (Troy Rutter)

Stamp kiosks are also great for getting other denominations of stamps. For 8x10 photos, after weighing my package on the scale with the photo, return envelope, letter, and a piece of cardboard, it usually comes out to $1.50. To be safe, I buy $1.60 stamps. Go to the kiosk, choose Buy Stamps, choose "Other Value," and then enter in $1.60. It will then ask how many you want and will dispense the stamps. Pretty cool! I also use the kiosk to buy larger value stamps for my "send" piece if I'm sending to Canada (usually $3.00) - but for the SASE I buy Canadian stamps directly from the Canada Post.

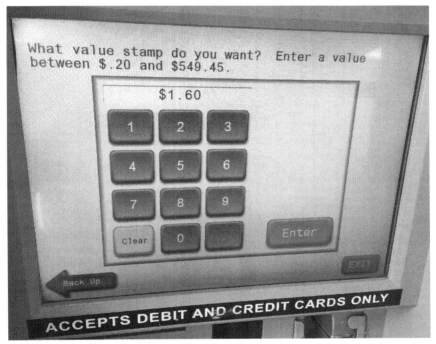

Purchasing a $1.60 stamp at a kosk. (Troy Rutter)

If you are mailing anything other than a letter, you can do that at the kiosk as well. The kiosk has rulers for measuring the package, as well as a scale to weigh it so you know the correct amount of postage and don't overspend. Since I tend to stick with regular envelopes for cards (Forever Stamps) and 8x10 photographs ($1.60 stamps), I very rarely use the kiosk for other things. But if you are doing trades or selling your collection, you definitely need to familiarize yourself with all the options, including insurance, at the kiosk.

Canadian Stamps

$5.00 in Canadian postage for international mail.

Oh, Canada… our home and native land! With Canada being so close to the United States, there are many TV and film celebrities (and studios) in that country, as well as sports teams. Oftentimes when researching your favorite TV show, you will find it films in Canada. You may think, "Great, that's more trouble than it is worth!" It does take a little bit of effort, but it is worth it. Sending to Canadian addresses has produced some of my highest success rates for TTMs, maybe because not many people go through the effort to find out how to do it properly.

To get TTM returns from Canada, you will need some Canadian stamps. It is actually quite easy to obtain these. All you need to do is order them directly from the Canada Post at *canadapost.ca*. On the website, you will find they sell what they call Domestic, US, and International stamps. Remember that this system is designed around those who actually *live* in Canada. Domestic stamps, therefore, are for sending a letter from Canada to someone else in Canada. US is for sending a standard letter from Canada to the US. International is for anywhere else other than the US.

If you are sending sports cards that fit in a standard #10 envelope, buy some of the "USA" stamps that come 50 on a roll at $1.20 each. Keep in mind, this is $1.20 in Canadian dollars, so it will be a little less than that when you actually purchase them from the US using a credit card - if the economy keeps up, that is! If you are going to be sending 8x10 photos, I recommend purchasing a roll of 50 International stamps at $2.50 each. I then use two of these stamps on the return envelope, for a total of $5. I haven't had one come back "postage due" yet.

Once you order your stamps, they will arrive in about a week and you will be ready to rock and roll!

UK And Other Stamps

On the rare occasion I send items to the UK, I buy stamps on eBay, or through one of the popular collecting forums. Any of the bigger forums will have a message board devoted specifically to trading stamps of one country or another. Just like in the US, these countries have different classes of mail, and hence different prices. Check out Appendix F for an entire reference on sending items back and forth between the US and the UK. The information is also great for other countries as well.

Pens and Sharpies

Some pens write better on specific cards. While it is more expensive to mail, many collectors will send a specific pen or sharpie along with their item for a celebrity to use, rather than relying on a celebrity having a pen that will work on the card or photo. In all my years of TTMing, I have only had a handful come back where the signature was bad because of a cheap pen. In one case, the pen used was obviously not a real sharpie or ballpoint, and it wiped completely off the card. Most celebrities know to sign items using sharpies (of varying tip sizes), so sending a pen of your own is really not necessary - but it is an option. If you do, you will want to use a bubble mailer to send your pen and card together, and don't expect the pen back.

"Do Not Bend" Stamps

Two popular pre-inked stamps for putting notes on envelopes.

This is a luxury supply item since you can always write "DO NOT BEND" on the envelope yourself. As with so many things in the hobby, these come in many styles and sizes. It doesn't matter which one you get, just be sure it is self-inking so you don't need a red ink pad. I like the large stamps that measure about 1" x 2 3/4", but I have also purchased some online by mistake that are smaller. While some people say postal carriers never actually see what is on the reverse side of the envelope, I always put a Do Not Bend stamp on the back of my sends and SASE's. If nothing else, it makes me feel better.

Air Mail Stamp

If you are sending from the US to another country, you might as well buy an Airmail/Por Avon stamp as well. It will save you time at the post office and let you drop them into the already-stamped bin.

Note Cards

Three-by-five-inch note cards are a popular item to send for TTMs, even though some celebrities never sign them for fear of their signatures being "lifted" to use on other documents or merchandise. While I formerly enclosed them in my sports card sends, I very rarely do so any longer. I do keep a supply ready just in case, and I also use them as extra padding in an envelope if I am only sending one card. If they come back signed, all the better!

PO Box

This one is really a "nice to have." I want to make sure the items I receive arrive in the best possible condition, so I rent a PO Box. If an item is too big for my PO box, it is kept at the front counter or put into a locked box where I can get it at my leisure. It also makes it a lot safer to publish my address on the Internet where people can make trades, send care packages, etc.

Cards

You can find trading cards for various sports at Walmart, Target, or just about any other major retailer. They will come in the form of regular packs, from gravity boxes, rack packs, and other various packaging. You can also find cards at The 99¢ Store and other discount stores. For my recommended places to buy quality cards, please visit the resources section on *ttmautograph.com!*

Shopping List

On the next page is a shopping list you can take to your favorite office supply store. For a complete list of the above products, with links where you can order them, be sure to visit my website at *ttmautograph.com.* As I mentioned, you can also start out smaller with only standard envelopes and a few stamps.

Shopping List

- 500 count #10 Envelopes
- 500 count #6 Envelopes
- 1 pack of return address labels
- 1 ream of computer paper
- 1 package of lined paper (8 1/2 x 11 or 5" x 8")
- 1 package of 3x5 notecards
- 1 package of gel pens (for writing)

I also offer an "Autograph Starter Pack" you can purchase via my website at *ttmautograph.com/starterpack*. It has a supply of #10 and #6 envelopes, a get-started guide, useful addresses, and more.

Now that you have your mailing supplies, what are you going to collect? Let's tackle that next.

CHAPTER 4
FINDING YOUR NICHE

I debated whether or not to include a short chapter on *what* to collect in this book. My fear is that people will read this chapter and think, "Oh, those are the only things I should collect, and I don't like any of them, so I guess I won't even try." That is definitely not the reason I am including this chapter. The following ideas are a starting point showing that, while there are some common items to collect, there are also other niches to consider as well. Let's look at some of the common major categories first.

Trading Cards

Trading cards are one of the least expensive ways to get started in TTM collecting. They are relatively cheap (the common ones anyway) and cost the least to send and receive back. But even within the niche of trading cards, you can break things down further into more specific areas.

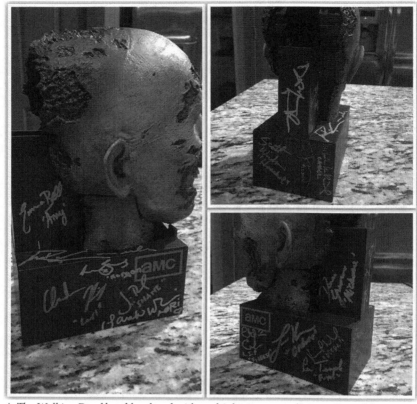

A *The Walking Dead* head bookend with multiple signatures (Jeremy Daniels)

Let's say you want to create a signed baseball card collection - one of the most common collections people have. You buy a few boxes of cards, and maybe some older complete sets, then sit down to figure out what to do next. Here is an example of what you could do to "niche down." The most general collection is at the top of the list, and the most specific one is at the bottom.

Baseball cards
   St. Louis Cardinals
     Pitchers/Catchers

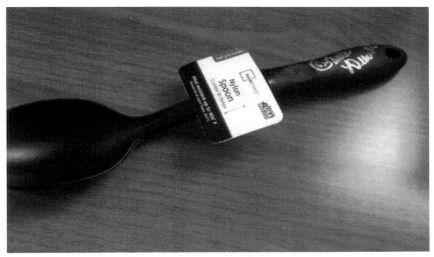

A cooking spoon signed by Paula Deen (Stacy Shaffer)

Baseball cards
> Jonathan Papelbon (Personal Collection or PC)

Baseball cards
> 1988-2008 All-Star game players

Each of these three ideas contains the top general category of baseball cards, but then begins to narrow things down. Some of the most common niches are to collect autographs or cards of a specific team or a player across many teams. These two types of collections are sometimes called a PC - a Personal Collection, something that you specialize in collecting. For instance, you may have a Denver Broncos PC, meaning you collect anything and everything related to the Denver Broncos (sports cards and other items).

TV and Film Niches

Taking a nod from the trading card niche, you can also find specific

Signed playing card from Kim Coates of *Sons of Anarchy* (Troy Rutter)

celebrities to collect. One of the most popular PCs in recent years has been the cast of *The Walking Dead*. In this type of collection, you may have trading cards, 8x10's, and other signed collectibles from the show. This can be a lot of fun, especially if there are many guest stars on a show so you get a steady influx of new possibilities for your collection. *Dexter* was another series many TTMers collected during the show's run.

Other Ideas

Looking beyond the traditional trading cards and 8x10 photos, you can try sending some other types of items to create a unique collection. Many of these require more money in postage since they are irregular sizes, but every success creates a new memory. Here are some examples I have seen over the past few years:

- Black cooking spoons with a silver sharpie - cooking show hosts.
- White thong underwear - adult film actresses (it's been done...)
- Red staplers - anybody from the film *Office Space*.
- Batting gloves - baseball players.
- Golf balls - professional golfers.

One contest I ran in 2016 involved sending a playing card to a celebrity to have signed, but it had to relate to the celebrity in some way. For instance, you could send a King or a Queen card to anymore on the TV show *King of Queens*. You could send a "5" to someone from the show *Babylon 5*, a "9" to someone from *Star Trek: Deep Space Nine*, or a Joker to a comedian. The goal was to build a full deck of cards, and we had some great returns. Everybody shared their successes with the community. A bonus with that type of a collection is that it could easily be stored in standard trading card binders. This type of collection is popular even without a contest, and there are thousands of different styles of trading cards you can use.

Printing Photos

Whether you collect TV, film, or sports celebrities on photographs, you will need a way to print them out so you have something to send. While some celebrities, such as Judith Light, will provide a photo if you ask, you can't rely solely on them to provide something of their own. It costs them money as well.

Printing your own photos at home is an option, although, in the long run, it could be more expensive than getting them professionally printed. In my experience, the best printers for printing photos at home are Canon PIXMIA printers, which use about six different colored inks to print on special photo paper. Canon also makes special glossy 8x10 photo paper that produces great results. Even though these look almost indistinguishable from traditional prints, they still are inkjet prints, so their color may begin to fade eventually, especially if left out in the sunlight.

A better alternative is to use a service to make actual photographs. I need to preface this by saying that images found on the Internet may be subject to copyright, so if you don't want to tiptoe on the line of legality, stop here and go to the next chapter on finding addresses. That being said, there are ways to get professional photos printed online, even if they are copyrighted.

First, search Google Images (*images.google.com*) for a celebrity. Under search options, be sure to choose a 2MP (megapixel) image or higher. Click on the image to go to the website it is on and right click to save the image to your computer. You can use your favorite image-editing program to adjust the photo to a size of 8" x 10" and at least 200 DPI.

Google imge search for George Clooney with "Larger than 2 MP" selected.

Once you have a bunch of photos saved (it is best to do many at the same time to save money on shipping costs), you can upload them to an online photo processor. My favorite at the time of this writing is called Sharp Prints at *sharpprints.com*. You can get an 8x10 photo for less than $1, typically around 80 cents each. Along the way, to cover themselves against lawsuits, they will ask you to confirm that you do in fact own the copyright to the photos you are uploading. I have yet to hear of a celebrity going after a fan for printing up a photo of them for their own use. That being said, it is up to you whether or not you want to say, "Yes, I own the copyright" or back out by saying, "No." Once your photos are uploaded, you complete the checkout process and your photos arrive via USPS in 3-5 days.

Home page of my favorite photo printing service, *sharpprints.com.*

You can also print out standard-size 4x6 photos the same way. Another popular site some people use is *snapfish.com.* They often have specials where you can buy 100 4x6 photos for a penny each.

One note: do not attempt to print out celebrity photos at a kiosk or online at Walmart, Costco, Target, or any self-service kiosk or photo development service. These types of photo-development places are trained to be very suspicious of the photos they print and will more than likely not print your photos for you. At the very least, they will make you sign a document saying you do own the copyright so they cover themselves legally. In my previous life as a publicist for a good many young actors, I took photos at charity events to use as headshots and other photos for autographs and magazine articles. I was grilled for several minutes about the photos I took, and was told they were "too good" and "too professional," so they refused to print them for me. After asking to speak to a manager (demanding, actually), I finally got them to print the photos, but only after they made me sign several documents attesting that I did in fact own the copyrights. Don't try it; it isn't worth the effort. You may have a good relationship with the local Costco or Walgreens, but in general my results have been very poor.

Custom Cards and Photos

You can also use your home printer to make custom cards and photos to send. Go to your favorite office supply store and look near the paper

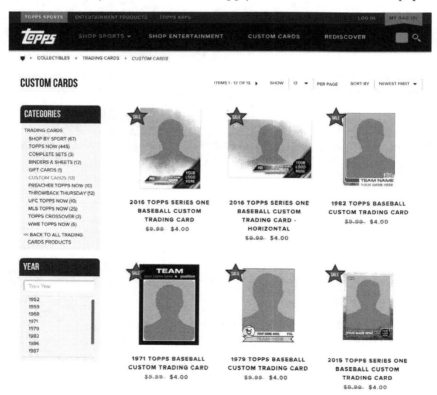

A variety of custom cards you can make at *Topps.com*.

aisle to find all of the assorted papers available. You will find brochure paper, postcards, invitations, and other sizes.

There are websites that allow you to print your own baseball cards, including Topps.com itself, but these tend to be very expensive, and you have to get multiple copies of the same card. If doing customs and one-offs, printing them as a traditional 4x6 photo, or using specialty papers from the office supply store, is highly recommended.

Blank Autograph Cards

There also websites online that sell special designs on cards made especially for autographs. The two most popular companies are *rackrs. com* and *theautographcard.com*. They have cards that are personalized for various sports teams, and also specialized cards. Whether you need

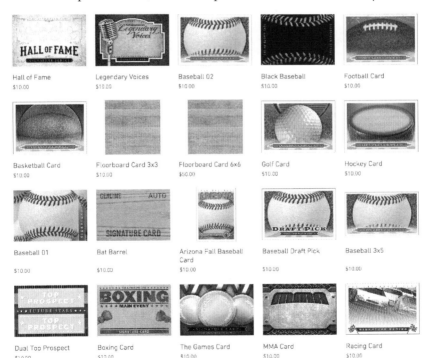

A variety of autograph cards available at *theautographcard.com*.

a card for a professional wrestler, voiceover actor, tennis pro, soccer star, or whatever, these two companies will probably have the perfect card for you. You can even use them at in-person events.

The backs of the cards have an area where you can write in the celebrity's name, claim to fame, where you got it signed, and the date. These cards are great to have handy if you don't have time to get a photo printed and you need something right away.

A custom baseball signature card from *facebook.com/HuyckGraphs*

Now that you have some ideas on what to collect and some supplies, let's get to one of the steps you will be doing a lot of in your autograph hunt: finding addresses.

CHAPTER 5

FINDING CELEBRITY ADDRESSES

Finding addresses for collecting autographs through the mail by itself isn't hard. Finding good, successful addresses, however, can be. Up until the mid 1990s, when the Web began to take shape, the only "reliable" address people had when writing to a celebrity was the production company for the movie or TV show they were on at the time. Countless letters were sent directly to Warner Bros., Disney, MGM, Universal, etc. Sometimes this worked, but many of the films were out of production by the time a letter would arrive, and autograph seekers would get the dreaded "Return to Sender" round-trip.

Sports addresses consisted mainly of writing via the stadium, and only during the regular season. Even then, sending your beloved baseball cards in the mail and hoping to get them back was not common among young collectors. Autograph inserts in packs were not invented yet, so the most common way to get your Cal Ripken, Jr. rookie card signed was to try and see him in person at a game.

As online resources such as Lexis Nexis became widely available, it got easier to search for a particular celebrity's representation. Suddenly you could search magazine articles and find out that Sean Connery was repped by XYZ management company. Aha! Another address to try.

Soon celebrity fan sites started popping up, and celebrities with only a few credits started Official Fan Clubs and websites where, for a fee, you could get a newsletter and an autographed photo from the source.

Fast-forward to today, when there are hundreds of different search engines and resources for finding the best address to write to your favorite celebrity or sports hero. Included in this chapter are some of my favorite resources --some well-known, and some tricks I have learned over the years to help you in your collecting.

Traditional Books

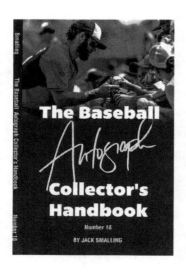

The Baseball Autograph Collector's Handbook, No. 18 by Jack Smalling Available on *Amazon.com* or at *baseballaddresses.com.*

Jack Smalling is the most trusted man in baseball autograph collecting, especially when it comes to addresses. Now in its 18th edition, the Baseball Autograph Collector's Handbook features over 13,350 names and over 8,000 addresses of baseball players from the 1930s to today. This latest edition contains over 89% of all addresses for living players. Even if you have a favorite online resource, the Smalling autograph books are required in any collector's library.

A little bit of trivia: I bought a house that Jack Smalling used to live in as my first house in Ames, Iowa. I thought it was unique that two collectors had both lived there. When I moved out, I learned the new owner is also an autograph collector. That house has some serious good autograph karma!

Stadium Addresses

Stadium addresses for your favorite sports players can be found via a simple internet search, but I have listed every stadium and pre-season venue in the back of this book for reference. These addresses are current as of 2016, but always double-check for the latest address by going to the website for your favorite team.

Movie Studio Addresses

Addresses of the major TV studios are also located in Appendix D at the back of this book. When watching a movie, you can find out the production companies by watching the opening credits (or just consult IMDb.com). Production and distribution companies for TV shows are usually appended to the end of a TV show's credits. If a TV show airs on The Disney Channel, you can guess what studio to look for if you can't find the specific address for a celebrity. You guessed it: Disney!

Online Address Resources

Fanmail.biz
Fanmail.biz

Fanmail.biz is one of the biggest, most popular free address resources on the Internet. They boast over 50,000 addresses for all kinds of celebrities. On a celebrity's page you will find one or more addresses, as well as any feedback from other users regarding the address. Fanmail.biz started in 2004 and has become a great resource. Successes are listed on a celebrity's page as a "feedback."

There is also a very active forum where you can discuss the authenticity of a signature, via-venue addresses, request an address, get tips on displaying or storing your collection, and more. Since it is a free site, there are a lot of banner advertisements, but the information itself is pretty solid. It is definitely a great resource.

Contact Any Celebrity
contactanycelebrity.com

Contact Any Celebrity (CAC) at *contactanycelebrity.com* is one of the oldest online resources. It started in 1996 and contains the addresses of over 59,000 celebrities. It is more expensive than other directories at $47 a month. Over the years, the site has received lots of positive press from newspapers and magazines, but it has slipped a little bit in terms of popularity. One of the reasons it has been so successful is that, in addition to the actual addresses it provides, it also has an affiliate program where website owners can make money referring people to their website. This promise of making money off recommending them has worked well, and they are indeed a great service if you can afford it.

Star Tiger
startiger.com

I have been a user of Star Tiger for many years, back to when they were called Star Archive. In terms of value and community, Star Tiger is my number one recommended resource for obtaining addresses of celebrities. The user interface used to be very clunky, but they have been working on rolling out improvements, especially over the past couple of years. The service only costs $4.99 a month, or you can buy a full year for $34.95. Definitely a bargain.

The community features of Star Tiger are a great bonus, but you don't have to participate in them to get the full value from the site. One of the most interesting features is the alerts and warnings on a celebrity listing page. These can show if a celebrity usually charges for an autograph (denoted by a green dollar sign), if the celebrity has passed away, or if the celebrity is suspected of using secretarial, preprints, or other fake autographs.

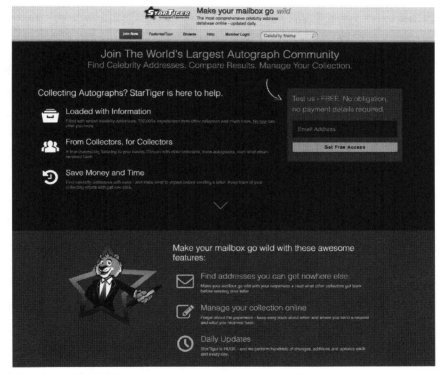

Home page of *startiger.com*.

One of the downfalls of Star Tiger is, since it is easy to use, there are collectors of various experience levels submitting successes without doing research. The site does not police its entries, so many secretarials and known autopens are often marked as "probably authentic" in the database. I don't have a solution for that except helping to educate collectors to do their research before submitting a success.

Sports Card Forum
sportscardforum.com

Sports Card Forum is a huge discussion message board dedicated to sports cards, and this includes great forums on through-the-mail autograph collecting. In the TTM section you will find forums such as "TTM Database," "Autograph Central," "TTM Archives," and "Memorabilia & Multi-Sport." You will also find forums dedicated to card collecting in general.

SportsCollectors.net
sportscollectors.net

SportsCollectors.net is another great resource if you are obtaining TTMs from sports celebrities. If you do a search for an athlete such as Billy Butler of the Kansas City Royals, you will get facts about the celebrity and also links on the left-hand side for viewing TTM addresses, or even when they might be doing a private signing. By creating an account you can also track your TTM sends and successes. A free membership lets you track your TTM submissions manually, but a paid subscription for only $15/year allows you access to the addresses themselves, as well as message boards and other community features.

A sister site to *SportsCollectors.net* is *sportscarddatabase.com.* This is one of my favorite sites for older baseball and football card requests. For example, let's say you had complete sets of 2007, 2008, and 2010 Topps baseball cards. You heard Billy Butler is a good signer, so you wanted to send him three different cards from those sets. Searching the internet (or manually) for his cards could take a long time. Instead, simply type in the player's name and it will tell you all of the card numbers in different sets for that particular player. You then pull those cards out of the sets, write your letter, and send them off. It is very fast and super easy. I highly recommend Sports Card Database if you have many sets close in years so you can send out multiple cards to players.

Advanced Tactics

One of my greatest frustrations with public sites, whether they are free or paid, is when some collectors put in "via venue" and do not share the actual address for fear that others will use it. Oftentimes, those that find a good address will "trade" the address for another exclusive or desired address. Personally, whenever I find a production address not listed, I will submit the address to the directory - period. As collectors, we must get over the fear of scarcity and embrace the idea of abundance. Sharing an address, especially one you have already written to (and hopefully received a return from), helps your fellow collectors.

The following resources are some of my favorite tools for finding addresses that may not yet be on Star Tiger or Fanmail.biz. It is important to have a personal toolbox you can consult if all else fails in your search.

Federal Elections Commission - Campaign Contributions
http://www.fec.gov/finance/disclosure/norindsea.shtml

Federal campaign financing regulations requires candidates to disclose any political contributions they receive. These contributions, and consequently the donors, are made public in a searchable database. While it is possible to use PO Boxes for an address when making a donation, many celebrities use their home address. Searching the database takes some sleuthing, as common names such as Steve Smith will pull up a lot of results. If you find a reliable address via this search, it is best to try and verify the address by some other advanced Google searching.

Home Sales

Home sales are another public source of information that can be used to find a celebrity's address. In addition to the actual home sale, newspapers sometimes run articles that mention a particular celebrity moving into the area. Doing an advanced internet search can sometimes provide clues as to these new addresses. For instance, if you know your favorite celebrity just moved to Toluca Lake, you can search for "_____ Toluca Lake" and see if it returns any results. You can get more keywords if you are a fan of the celebrity and notice any clues they post on social media to help narrow the search.

California Company Search
http://kepler.sos.ca.gov/

Many celebrities form companies to enjoy the tax benefits of being a corporation or LLC. Because these are actual legal entities registered with the state of California, they are able to be searched. Oftentimes, celebrities use a lawyer or a PO box as their address for their companies, but many use their home address.

Thats Them
thatsthem.com

This was a new one for me when I sat down and started writing this section of the book, but after a few simple searches for addresses of celebs I knew, the results were pretty good. You can search by name, phone number, email address, and more. It isn't 100% (my email address was given for a guy in Pennsylvania and a woman in Illinois), but the site did pull up about 99% of those that I searched for. It is definitely worth a try.

Production Listings

Finding the latest production field offices for movies and television is hit-or-miss with regular search engine searching. In addition, other resources for industry personnel, such as SAG-AFTRA, IATSE, etc., often don't have the most detailed information. There are several services designed to provide up-to-date production lists of films and TV shows.

Below the Line
findfilmwork.com
$15/month.

The best database I have found for production listings (film/TV) is Below the Line. For $15/month you have access to a wealth of information about the latest projects filming around the world. Plus, you can even add notes and reminders to notify you when something is changed or a certain title is added.

Fifteen dollars a month may sound a little pricey, but if you are an avid autograph collector, it is an invaluable resource, and one I highly recommend.

Below_{the}Line   *Jump to* ●   Log In | 💬 Support | ❓ FAQ | BTLNews

Current stats:

Production Listings: **22,839** listed projects | BTL News: **27,510** registered users
BTL411: **17,307** vendors in BTL411 Vendors & **2,186** crew resumes in BTL411 People

Below the Line News

Below the Line's editorial is the Voice of the Crew. Sign up for our daily news blast today. If you have a story that needs to be heard email scott.lehane@btlnews.com For advertising and sponsorship opportunities, please email dan.evans@btlnews.com. We have advertising plans to fit every budget.

Below the Line Screening Series

Sign up today for Below the Line's Award Season Screening Series and get invited to screenings, Q & A's and special events. Participants are vetted and must be working in the industry. For questions, please contact Dorothea Sargent at screenings@btlnews.com

Below the Line's Production Listings

Our Production Listings are the premier listings service in the industry. Listings are updated daily in a searchable database available to you 24/7. Set up saved searches with email notifications and make private notes directly in your account. Pay monthly or annually. Union/Guild Discounts available. Click here for samples and to subscribe now.

BTL411 Vendors

List the basics of your business for free in a searchable database available to your customers 24/7 from anywhere in the world. For $100 annual, move your listing to the top of your department and expand your image to include your website, logo, photos and PDF's to provide a better connection with your customers. BTL 411 People- List your credits, upload PDF's of your resume and use this as your website to showcase your work. In a searchable database available 24/7 from anywhere in the world. Questions please email patrick.graham@btlnews.com.

© 2018 Below the Line

Home page of Below the Line at *findfilmwork.com*.

Production Weekly
productionweekly.com
$75/month.

Production Weekly is a weekly publication (hence the name) that details the latest production locations throughout the United States. It costs $75/month, although the first month is discounted.

Production Alert
productionalertusa.com
$59.95/month.

Production Alert is another film and television production newsletter that lists projects currently in production or pre-production. For $59.95/month, you receive a newsletter organized into brand-new projects entering pre-production, feature projects in production, and projects in pre-production, with noted updates from the previous week.

By using any of these online resources, or even the stadium address in the back of this book, you will be able to find the addresses of the majority of celebrities, politicians, and athletes you are looking to collect. Be creative, and if you don't find an address you are looking for, ask for help on one of the forums or Facebook groups.

Once you have a list of potential addresses you want to try, the next step is crafting your actual through-the-mail package!

CHAPTER 6

THROUGH-THE-MAIL (TTM) COLLECTING

Through-the-mail (TTM) collecting is a fun way to acquire autographs of your favorite sports and TV/film celebrities, no matter where you live. You don't have to be near a major sports stadium or in a large city to get autographs from your favorite players. You simply write a letter, send your item in the mail, and patiently wait for its return. Instead of bills in your mailbox every day, you will look forward to your latest self-addressed stamped envelopes (SASE) to arrive...or cringe if you see a yellow "forwarding order expired" sticker, signaling that the item has returned unsigned.

Once you have all your supplies (you did stock up, right?), and your web browser is open to your favorite online address resources, you are finally ready to put pen to paper (or fingers to keyboard). There are different approaches to creating your letters of request (LOR), depending on who you ask.

Letter of Requests

Whether to handwrite or type up your LOR has been a subject of debate among hobbyists for years. There is no definitive answer. When I started collecting autographs, I wrote each one out by hand on college-ruled notebook paper to show the celebrity how much of a fan I truly was. After all, everybody knows writing a letter by hand takes time. I started getting items returned signed, but some people also returned my original handwritten letter! The celebrity may not have even read it, and if they did, they apparently didn't want to keep it. It was after this happened several times that I decided to make the following rules for my collecting:

1. If it is a celebrity I truly admire and I would really cherish their autograph, I handwrite my LOR.

2. If I am merely filling in a spot in my collection, or have only a casual interest in a celebrity, I type the letter.

3. If I do a "beast mode" mass sending of TTMs, then these are typed into a form letter for the team with little personalization.

As with everything in the TTM world, opinions on handwriting your LOR or typing them vary widely. If you search on YouTube for "letter of request autograph" you will get several pages of videos promising "the right way" to compose your letters of request. Over time you will develop your own system and preferred method.

If I do hand-write my LOR, I usually use a pad of paper that is smaller than normal notebook paper, such as a 6"x9" pad. This means I don't have to write as much to make it look like the entire page is full. A LOR has the following basic content:

- Date
- Your Address
- Celebrity's Address
- Introductory Paragraph
- Paragraph about why you like the celebrity
- The actual request
- Thanks for their time
- Your signature

Below is an example LOR that I might use to write to the star of *Dexter*, Michael C. Hall.

August 29, 2016

J Random Fan
5555 Fandom Blvd.
Imafan, MT 33995

Michael C. Hall
c/o Authentic Talent And Literary Management
45 Main St, Ste 1004
Brooklyn, NY 11201

Dear Mr. Hall,

Hello! My name is J Fan and I just moved to MT after living in FL for most of my life. I have to admit I missed a lot of Dexter when I was in college, so thanks to Netflix I am catching up by binge-watching everything I missed. I am really enjoying it!

I had the chance to see your play Lazarus in New York about a year ago when I was visiting my sister in New York. I heard you are now performing in London? It must be interesting to do the same play thousands of miles away. I meant to try and get my playbill signed at the theatre, but all I could attend was a matinee and I was told the cast didn't sign between those.

I am hoping you might have time to please sign a photo for me? I would really appreciate it and would mean a lot. I printed it out from a file I found on the Internet. I am also including a Dexter DVD cover I had from the first season.

Thank you for the great performances and for all your work with the Leukemia & Lymphoma Society. It is so great you support a charity enough to be a spokesperson. I am sure they appreciate it.

Thank you again, and I hope to hear from you soon.

J Fan

You will notice I start the letter with an introduction, tell an interesting anecdote about the celebrity or how I relate to them and enjoy their work, ask for an autograph, and then thank them for their time. All of my autograph requests revolve around the same basic LOR template.

For trading cards, I sometimes try and include an anecdote about the last game before I wrote the letter. For instance, "That was a tough game when you lost to XXX yesterday." An example of a trading card LOR follows.

September 11, 2016

J Random Fan
5555 Fandom Blvd.
Imafan, MT 33995

Michael Thomas
c/o New Orleans Saints
5800 Airline Drive
Metairie, LA 70003

Dear Mr. Thomas,

Are you ready for some foooooootball? I've been singing that song since I was little and I am really stoked about the rest of the season this year! I can't wait to see what the Saints can accomplish this season - I am sure it is going to be great!

I am writing this to you after that heartbreaking loss to the Raiders today - that game really came down to the wire! You all did everything you could to win that game - and that 2 point conversion was awesome! I am sure you will rebound quickly and rise to the top!

I was wondering if you could please sign a card for me? I picked up a few packs at the store and was thrilled to see you were one of the players in the pack. It would really mean a lot to me - who knows, I could be your good luck charm this season!

Thank you so much and I hope the rest of the season is a winning one!

Your fan,

J Fan

I admit that I often use the same "form letter" when I send trading cards because it saves time. I used to think players would be upset over getting a form letter if they saw a guy at the next locker over receive nearly the same thing. Imagine that for a second, though. You're in the locker room after a game or practice. An athlete's fan mail for the week is sitting on the counter in the main part of the locker. He and his teammates have just showered, sit down, and start opening their fan mail. One leans over to the teammate next to him and says, "Josh Greenblood sent you the same letter? He's not getting my autograph!" He then throws it into the trash.

Not a likely scenario, is it?

Professional athletes do not sit around the locker room and open up their fan mail together, sharing them with other players. If they are going to throw their mail into the trash, they go into the bin then and there. The majority of athletes who will sign, take them home, sign them, and then drop them off at the team office or in a post office blue box themselves. You are not going to get a bad rep for sending the same letter to the whole team at once. However, it may be better to spread out your sends to an entire team over the course of several weeks, just so the person sorting the mail doesn't see them all at once and suspect you are a dealer, only looking for things to sell.

Whether you send a typed letter or a handwritten one, be sure to sign your letter of request. If you type your letter, include a short handwritten note at the bottom. I always sign my TTM LOR in blue ink, so the celebrity knows it wasn't just printed and photocopied/mail merged. If you provide your real signature, maybe they will too!

If sending trading cards, do *not* send them in penny sleeves or top loaders. Over the years I have seen many reports of athletes signing the top loader or penny sleeve without taking the card out, leaving the signature on the plastic and not the card! You can still protect the card by placing it between cardboard or index cards (IC's) inside the envelope.

When I first started with TTMs, I used this method and received some of the IC's back signed as well.

Card Prepping

Unprepped Topps Chrome - notice the bubbling and streaking in the signature? (Troy Rutter)

A by-product of the latest trading-card production process has resulted in premium trading cards on very slick cardstock. In addition, certain brands are known to practically refuse to take on ink from even the best Sharpies. Think of it as using a dry erase marker and board - the signature wipes right off. There are a few tricks you can do to help the signature on these cards stay bold and not "bubble" or streak.

The first method is simply rubbing the card where the person might sign with your thumb. This takes off some of the shine, and leaves some of your oils on the card as well. The second method is using a white eraser and literally erasing the prime signature area of the card. You can then use your thumb to remove all the little eraser bits. Finally there is a more messy way: using baby powder. Sprinkle baby powder on the card, rub it in a little, and then wipe off with a clean cloth. Personally, I prefer simply not sending chrome cards at all and sticking with older cards, regular Topps or Topps Heritage to avoid the problem altogether.

Beast Mode

A couple of pages ago, I mentioned the term "beast mode." This is a slang term I use when describing how I ramp up my TTM sends, usually to an entire team at the same time. Let's say the Vikings just lost a game. In my letter, I change the recipient, but the rest of the letter is exactly the same. I might say, "That was a great game against the _____" or "I'm writing this letter off the heartbreaking loss to _____." Everything about the letter is the same for everyone on the team, with no special anecdotes about a specific player. I usually then mail out 3-4 a day over the course of a week or two. This is a way to blanket an entire team quickly.

What Not To Say In Your LOR

I hate including this section in this book, but some things need to be said. For most people, this section is common sense, but there are some who simply do not show common decency and their LOR crosses a line of what is appropriate. Over the years as a publicist for several actors, I have seen LORs come in that were rude, crude, disrespectful, and just plain weird. Please keep your LOR courteous and G-rated. After all, celebrities are communicating with their fans on their own time, and for the most part, they enjoy interacting with the lives they are touching through their talents.

Do not ask for any sort of DNA through hair, skin samples, shavings, or other biological matter. You may think I am joking, but there was a certain fan in the late 1990s who was well known among my clients and other performers for asking for hair samples so they could clone the celebrity once technology improves. Don't be that person.

Do not include anything in your LOR that is sexual in nature. Period. You may be sending a photograph of an adult film star in various degrees of undress, but your letter should remain polite and never ask for any "favors" from the celebrity - other than an autograph.

Do not mention how you looked up their address and took a trip to Los Angeles last month and noticed they bought a new car, but you are not sure what the license plate letters spell. This is cause for alarm for any celebrity. Don't be the guy who shows up on TMZ with a restraining order against them.

In general, be courteous. A celebrity doesn't have to sign autographs. They are doing it because they want to give back to their fans. Be a fan, not a stalker.

Sending Multiple Items

Some experts in the TTM community recommend sending only one item with each request. I followed this approach for years, all the while seeing others sending and receiving two, even three items at a time. On tracking sites such as Star Tiger, it is easy to see how many items celebrities are signing by looking for the stats such as 1/2 or 2/3. This means the celebrity signed 1-of-2 or 2-of-3 respectively. You will also see if they sent 2 cards and only 1 was returned, such as "signed 1, kept 1."

You can safely send three (3) trading cards with one U.S. first-class Forever Stamp. Anything more than that and you may want to weigh the envelope at the post office to get exact postage, or put 2 Forever stamps on both the send and the SASE. As a general rule, I rarely send more than 3 cards at a time. In addition, if sending 3 cards, I try to make sure the cards are different. I never send 3 of the same card as that seems greedy to me. If I was the one receiving that package, I would only sign one, because the person requesting 4 of the same card might be selling them. Try and mix things up.

Sending Via Venue

Sending a TTM Via Venue is sending to a non-permanent location you know a celebrity will be at for a certain amount of time. Some of the most popular via venue addresses are via Broadway shows in New

York, many of which will provide signed playbills of the cast without a fee. (Note: There is an increasing trend for some shows to require a donation to charity in exchange for a signed playbill.) Other via venue ideas include award shows or fundraisers, movie set addresses, or even hotels if you know a certain celebrity will be staying or performing there.

The same rules apply to via venue TTMs as with any other TTM, although with via venue, timing is of the essence. For instance, if you know George Clooney is going to be at a certain fundraiser in September, you will want to get your item there in plenty of time. Just like regular TTMs, there are no guarantees you will get something back, but there are ways to help increase your odds if you follow certain guidelines.

First, make sure your item arrives at the location about a week before the event if it occurs on one specific day. If you send it too soon, it has a greater chance of getting lost or misplaced. If you sent it too late, especially for Broadway shows and movie shooting locations, it may not get sorted and delivered in time to make it to the celebrity. In that case, it will either go in the trash or be returned to you with the dreaded "RTS" on the envelope.

For Broadway shows, be sure you send at least two weeks before the show closes. This will allow enough time for your request to be processed, and if there are any signed playbills available you will have a good chance at getting one returned. I once wrote Linda Lavin a little too close to her show closing on Broadway. I sent a photo to be signed, but it didn't arrive until the show closed. The venue returned my item unsigned, which I was at first upset about, but when I looked closer I found they had included a signed playbill they had left over! It isn't the same as a signed photo, but it was nice of them. When a show closes, sometimes there are signed playbills left over, but most of the time once a show closes your late items will just be returned unsigned.

On the popular address sites such as Star Tiger and Sports Card Forum, many via venue addresses are kept a secret. You will see a "via venue" notice and pending submissions, but there won't be an address listed. This is common, and although I personally don't agree with the scarcity mentality some people seem to have when it comes to addresses ("I won't tell you the address because then you might get something I don't!"), I don't dwell on it. I spend a little time sleuthing and I can usually find the address. If I am feeling particularly ornery, I will then submit that address to the website as a temporary address so others can write the celeb as well - just to spite the people trying to keep the address to themselves.

Sending expensive items to an address via venue is not recommended due to the chance of them not being returned. I have tried George Clooney several times over the years and he still eludes me. The photo I would like signed is very specific, so I ordered a few extra from my online printer just in case I have the opportunity to try a few more. Best advice I can give for via venue successes is the same as with any TTM send - don't send anything irreplaceable.

Tracking Your Sends

Before you mail your package off to the celebrity, be sure to record the details of what you are sending and when. You can do this in a spreadsheet, including the columns:

- NAME
- DATE SENT
- ADDRESS SENT TO
- ITEM DESCRIPTION
- NUMBER OF ITEMS
- DATE RECEIVED.

These are the basic columns you need, but you can include others. If sending cards, you can get very detailed in your description. If using Star Tiger or another service, you can find the "Add Pending" button on a celebrity's page, next to the address, and add your information there.

Keeping track of your LOR sends is fun and highly recommended.

Waiting

This is the hardest part for any TTMer - the wait. Sometimes you will only wait a few days for a return; sometimes it will be a few years. You may also never get a response at all. Or, you might get one of those massive mail days like Zane Savage once had, where the post office delivered his mail in an actual giant mailbag!

J.J. Watt TTM return from 2012. (Troy Rutter)

The only real way to increase your success rate is to be very careful and only send to celebrities who have a proven track record for returning TTMs. While this seems like a good strategy, it also severely impairs your chance at a receiving a one-in-a-million success. A few years ago, I sent some cards off to Texans football star JJ Watt, who even then was top football rookie.

They came back signed and are some of my most prized TTMs. In 2015, I sent off to baseball player Jonathan Papelbon. His history on Star Tiger was pretty bad, with items typically returned unsigned or not returned at all. For some reason, during 2015 Spring Training, he started returning cards signed and I was thrilled when I received 3/3 from him. The autograph community was also surprised - and people began talking about it. I was skeptical but did the research and everything looks good.

Fan Packs

Fan packs are literature many teams send out instead of forwarding your mail to a particular player, or even to fans asking specifically for them. They are also sent to a fan if a player requests the front office not deliver fan mail. Instead, the front office enters your name and address

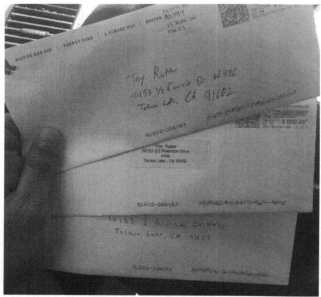

3 fan packs in a day from the Boston Red Sox. (Troy Rutter)

into a database and sends you a fan pack. The postage on the fan pack oftentimes exceeds the postage of the item you sent. Fan packs usually contain a team schedule, a letter saying the sports figure is too busy to sign, sometimes a pre-printed autograph, and a logo sticker or team photo. The top teams I usually receive fan packs from are the Boston Red Sox and the New York Yankees. As much as I hate fan packs, I keep trying those teams in hopes of getting a hit. In 2016 I received 3 fan packs from the Boston Red Sox in a single day. Fan packs are easily spotted in your mailbox since they usually have the team's logo on the envelope and are easily distinguishable from your SASE.

Request for Donation

Another common TTM failure is when an item comes back with a request for a donation to a charity the celebrity endorses, or sometimes even just a request for a check written out to the celebrity. Wade Boggs, for example, returns every regular TTM unsigned, but if you include $5 per item, he will sign. Some teams will enlist the majority of their roster with a charity program. The Detroit Tigers have nearly all of their players signed up to request $20 or more for each signed item. While I applaud teams like the Tigers for raising money for their charity, as a TTMer and fan, sometimes it is very disappointing.

Standard "Autographs for a Cause" letter from the Detroit Tigers.

The "Successful" Return

Getting your item back in the mail is a great feeling. You can't wait to rip it open, see what came in, then hop on the Internet to see how long it took and if other people are getting the same results. Sometimes, however, items are returned in your SASE unsigned and with no explanation. One of the most dreadful feelings is opening up your SASE expecting to find a good return, only to find your cards returned unsigned, or worse, a letter saying they will gladly sign it for a fee.

If you do get an autograph returned successfully - congratulations! The next thing to do is to try and compare the signature. You can find some tips on verifying your signature's authenticity in the chapter "Real or Fake." In general, you can use Google image search to try and validate if the signature looks like other ones people have acquired in person. Look at the autograph strokes - are they smooth or choppy? In the following chapter, I will share some secrets on how to determine if a signature is real or fake. In reality, there is no way to be 100% certain. In fact, there are some collectors who automatically discount any autograph returned TTM as fake. Period.

Now there is some optimism for you!

In my experience, about 95% or more sports-related TTMs returned appear authentic. This higher percentage is because sports figures tend to simply not return an item at all if they don't want to sign. TV and film celebrities, politicians, and astronauts, on the other hand, tend to employ other means such as autopen machines, secretaries, managers, husbands, wives, brothers, sisters, friends, etc., to help them sign autographs. Because of this, my personal experience with returned TTMs from non-sports celebrities is more around 80-85% authentic.

Bottom line: DO YOUR RESEARCH. Check out other autographs that are posted online and compare them.

Does everything look good? Congratulations, you just received another successful TTM return! Now, get that next LOR out and keep going!

Google image search for "Pete Rose autograph" (*images.google.com*)

CHAPTER 7
REAL OR FAKE?

The subject of authenticity is a divisive one in the autograph community. Ask five different experts about the authenticity of a particular signature and you are likely to get split opinions on whether it is real or fake. There are some who consider *any* TTM return inauthentic just to avoid the hassle of confirming TTMs altogether.

One thing is for certain - the only 100% authentic autograph is one obtained in person. But even if you *do* have photo proof, you are not exempt from having your beloved signature questioned by experts and appraisers. Even experts can be wrong.

Friends on social media will sometimes turn on each other if one of them mentions a return is probably fake or secretarial. I have seen online communities become fragmented over the mere accusation or even hints that their latest autograph isn't real.

Let's take a look at some of the "easy" ways to determine if an autograph is real or fake, and follow that up with a subject that always comes up - third-party authenticators. Please keep in mind that just doing a google search does not provide conclusive results. Authenticating autographs is both an art and a skill. These are meant mainly to help identify the most common fakes.

Obvious Fakes

Obvious fakes and forgeries hit the auction sites and hobby stores all the time. Obvious fakes oftentimes share one characteristic: it is physically impossible for an autograph to exist on the item in question.

Consider a Babe Ruth autograph - one of the most commonly forged baseball autographs in history. You have to perform some very careful research if you are authenticating his signature. I wouldn't even try! But what if the autograph is on a brand new, pristine baseball the collector says has been kept in argon gas since before Ruth died in 1948?

In this example, it sounds impressive and maybe even believable, but argon isn't known for its ability to shield a baseball from the effects of time. In addition to this, we look closely and notice the baseball itself is manufactured to modern standards and clearly wasn't made until long after 1948.

Another example is when new cards are printed that look like the old version of a card. Many of the big trading card companies create reprints of older cards to insert in packs, including big league greats. Scammers may fake an autograph on such a card, not seeing the tiny print on the reverse that reveals the copyright date is actually after the player died. Or, the company itself may embed a subtle difference in the card that only experts know about in an attempt to thwart scammers.

Do Your Own Research

When you receive a signature through the mail, the first thing you should do is your own research. If you subscribe to Star Tiger, go into the gallery for the particular celebrity and look at "In Person" signatures, comparing those to the one you received. Sometimes there are vast differences between in-person and through-the-mail autographs, but you should be able to find examples of both to compare with yours. Comparing TTM signatures to on-card signature autos is more reliable. You should be careful if you compare other TTM signatures and find they match yours -- it does not mean they are authentic.

If the same secretary or person signs every single TTM request a celebrity receives, then your autograph will *still* match all of the others. Obviously, this doesn't mean it is authentic. For instance, the same secretary was reportedly known to sign for Robin Williams for over 20 years. If you look up the photo gallery for a celebrity on Star Tiger, you will see numerous photos, all looking the same, and all marked as "Probably Authentic." People just didn't do the research and marked them as probably authentic.

Which brings up an important point: Don't take the word of other collectors, or if you do, be sure to do your own research to confirm. Despite good evidence, most TTM autographs for Carrie Fisher of *Star Wars* are secretarial. New "successes" added to the site by a TTM collector are often marked as "Probably Authentic." This is amazing considering Star Tiger has a call-out on the page saying, "This celebrity is suspected of using secretarial signatures."

> **Note:**
>
> Added By Starc on 2015/02/02
>
> There are discussions that this celebrity might use an autopen, pre-prints or secretary for at least some TTM autographs (You might find more info in the forum section).

StarTiger.com notice that a celebrity is suspected of sending secretarials.

If you do not subscribe to StarTiger (and you really should…), there is another way to gather research on a particular celebrity's scribble. Go to Google image search at images.google.com and search for your celebrity's name and the words "autograph" or "signed." Here are some examples:

- "Mark Hamill" signed
- "Mark Hamill" autograph

A short side note: I highly recommend doing the above image search when you have a couple of moments. Mark has signed some pretty awesome autographs and sayings onto trading cards over the years.

Remember as always to do your own research when going through the resulting images from this search. There could still be some fakes mixed in with the real ones.

The bottom line in this section of authenticating your own TTMs is to Do the Research. Do not get caught up in the moment and mark your "success" as such without checking it out first. There will always be some questionable returns, such as Tom Selleck, whose signatures many believe are all secretarials. Simply comparing in-person and authenticated should give you an idea whether it is an outright secretarial or a "probably authentic."

Please do the autograph world a favor and do not mark something as probably authentic before you do research. I beg you.

Re-prints and Preprints

Reprints and preprints are similar but slightly different. Preprints are often mailed out by the celebrity themselves to fans requesting an autograph. These are photos where the signature is actually in the photo. In other words, the celebrity signed the photo and then they made duplicates of those signed photos. A reprint is more or less the same, but these are usually used by people selling autographs for profit. You should

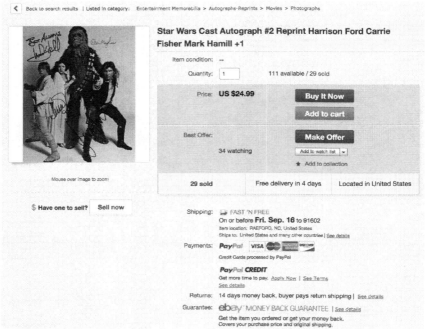

Harrison Ford, Carrie Fisher, and Mark Hamill Reprint - only $25! (ebay.com)

be aware that many of the "signed" photos you see on eBay, especially the lower-priced ones, are actually reprints or preprints. If you dig deeper into the descriptions, you will see something like:

> "Harrison Ford and Mark Hamill personally signed photo RP! - $29!"

The price is a definite giveaway. Also notice the abbreviation RP in the listing. The casual eBay buyer wouldn't know RP stands for "reprint." Even though the seller in this case did use the abbreviation "RP" for reprint, they included misleading language about it being "personally signed." Yes, the original photograph of Mark and Harrison was personally signed - once. Now it is being mass-produced to try and fool the casual fan. Be careful out there!

Who would buy a preprint or a reprint intentionally? Believe it or not, some people do. Maybe you are remodeling your basement into a home theater and want some "signed" movie posters or photos to decorate the space. Or maybe you are opening a 1950s-style restaurant and you want signed photos of actors, actresses, and musicians from the period. There is a market, somewhere, for preprint and reprint photos - but not for the collector.

How can you tell if the photo you have is a reprint or preprint? First, if you bought the photo online and it has the acronyms RP or PP in the description, that is a clear indication. It can also be a bit trickier. The first thing is to look at images of other people's TTM returns, similar to what we have already discussed. Look at your photo and their photo and see if it contains the same inscription in relatively the same place and spacing. We will talk about this later on when it comes to autopens as well. But if it is the same exact photo and the signature is in the same exact place and looks the same - chances are it is a RP or PP.

Another way to look for signs of a preprint is to carefully inspect the autograph's finish. Hold the photo close to your eye by a light and tilt it away from you slightly. Try to see differences in the photo's finish and the signature. If the signature is real, most sharpie markers will turn a purplish color (even the black ones) when tilted in this manner. If your photo has a semi-gloss surface, you can oftentimes discover a reprint by actually seeing the signature below the finish of the photo. You can also look for various indentations on the surface. Look on the back of the photo near the signature to try and find and indentations from the pen the celebrity was using. This will help you rule out a PP or RP, but you will still have the challenge of authenticating secretarial or autopen.

Another way I have seen reprints ruled out is by using a dab of rubbing alcohol on a cotton swab and lightly dabbing a small piece of the signature. If some of the ink comes off, then it is at least a real signed photo and not a RP or PP. Again, you still need to authenticate though. I should warn you, this method may damage the photo, so I would use it as a last resort.

Autopens

The use of autopens, or "robot pens" as they were first called, has still not gone out of style. The term autopen is actually a name for a device used to sign documents and manufactured by The Autopen Company. As is the case of Xerox for copiers, the name has become commonplace to describe any machine use to duplicate a signature or block of writing.

An autopen uses consistent pressure and angle, using a pen, sharpie, or other writing instrument. Early autopens used an engraved wheel or plate for the signature itself, which was then connected to an arm (or arms) and a stylus to reproduce a signature. Newer autopens can process a signature scanned and placed on an SD card or a USB stick directly into the machine. The signature is then converted into a template to control the stylus and sign anything needed. While the first autopens were relegated to signing paper items and documents because the machines were big and cumbersome, modern autopens can sign a variety of items, including baseballs, footballs, jerseys, and more.

Autopens were first used by presidents and politicians, but because of their popularity, they have been adopted by sports and movie personalities as well. The autopen is also a favorite among astronauts and military officers.

Modern autopens are getting more sophisticated, but there are still ways to tell them apart from real signatures. One of the easiest ways, especially for older autopens, is to carefully examine the signature itself. Look for two main things: jaggedness of the signature, and also the width (pressure) of the signature. Many autopens appear "jaggy" because the pen starts and stops along the template, making the ink "pool" out longer along the stops. This gives a subtle appearance of "connecting the dots" if you look carefully. In addition, the start of strokes will appear abnormally large where the pen first touches the paper.

Similarly, when a real person signs an autograph, the pressure differs as they sign and move their hand over the item. In an autopen, the pressure is always the same. If the sharpie line width is exactly the same throughout the whole signature, that is a good indication of an autopen.

I have been fooled by an autopen myself. When I worked with performers in the 1990s, I routinely saw actor Shia LaBeouf at events and signings, but I never asked for an autograph. A couple of years ago, I decided to try and get an autograph after one of the Transformers movies was released. I sent my photo to a private address and waited. I also included a very personal letter detailing specifics from when we used to hang out. I got it back signed and was ecstatic. I posted my success on the Internet, and then I got a dreaded response from one of my friends.

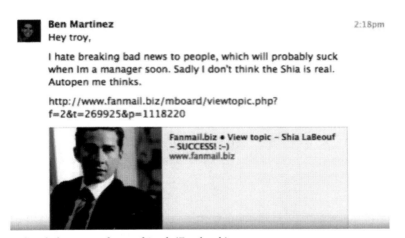

A dreaded message from a friend. (Facebook)

Remember how I mentioned that people get upset over others pointing out a precious autograph may be fake? Well, I wasn't too happy. But, I did the research and looked up a signature from Shia on the internet and found that, yes, several signatures looked very similar, including the inscription. I opened both signatures in Photoshop and laid one over the other. Sure enough, they matched up exactly. I then went onto my Facebook page and told everyone it was an autopen after all.

After that public admission, I decided I wanted to help educate others in the community by doing a video that showed my process of discovering and confirming the fake signature.

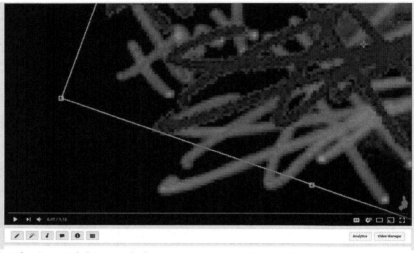

A video I created showing Shia's autopen signature. (YouTube)

Third Party Authenticators

Sometimes what seems like a good thing -- having a neutral, third-party expert authenticate signatures -- still manages to create controversy. In the collecting world, there are stories all the time about how an authentic item didn't pass third-party authentication, or where an obvious forgery passed inspection. Conspiracy theorists have long made accusations that many dealers are in league with authenticators to pass their items as authentic and their competitors' items as fakes. While I am sure mistakes are made from time to time, I have to believe that authenticators strive to make the correct analysis as often as possible. Yes, there may be some "bad apples" out there, but they are hopefully few and far between.

In researching this book, I spoke to workers from an autograph shop in Las Vegas who specialize in framing autographs, and who also arrange public signings with celebrities. They told me of a signing they set up with Michael Jackson. One woman had a black fedora signed by the King of Pop, and they even had a picture of him signing the item. When she sent it to the authenticator, it came back as a forgery. The woman knows it is authentic and she has photo proof. Could she have mass produced fakes after getting the photos? Possibly. Is it probable? The likelihood in this case is simply that the authenticators made a mistake. It happens.

The most popular and well-known authenticators are PSA/DNA and JSA. When you see a baseball or football card encapsulated in a plastic case, with a number grading on top with a bar code, chances are it was PSA/DNA or JSA certified. Each authenticator offers its own set of features for the price of submitting an item for grading and authentication.

PSA/DNA
psacard.com

PSA/DNA provides several services, including card grading and a condition rating ranging from 1-10, as well as autograph authenticity and grade of the autograph itself. They also offer a service called crossover grading if the card had been graded by another authenticator such as JSA. For trading cards, you can have only the card graded, or both the card and the autograph graded and authenticated.

For instance, say you are a big Fernando Valenzuela fan. You have a photo of both him and Tommy Lasorda you want authenticated. If you only had Fernando Valenzuela, you could search the PSA/DNA website and learn that it would cost $20 (plus shipping, etc.) to have the photo authenticated. If you only had Tommy Lasorda, it would be $25. If you had them both, that would be a multi-signed item, with Tommy Lasorda (as the highest value) being the primary signer. The fee, according to the chart at the time of printing, would be $35. (So, $25 for Lasorda, $10 for the additional Valenzuela.)

For non-sports cards such as photos, it can get a little tricky. On the PSA/DNA website there is a fee schedule you can search through to find the cost of having your particular item authenticated. Some celebrities will be pricier than others. Items sent in for this kind of authentication can be photos, jerseys, baseballs, footballs, mini helmets, etc. Pricing gets more complicated in the case of multi-signed items.

Detailing the intricacies of baseball autograph grading and PSA/DNA pricing would take a book onto itself, and it would be instantly out of date after publishing. The best way to find out pricing for either grading or authenticating your item is to use the fee calculator on their website at *http://www.psacard.com/services/tradingcardgrading*.

JSA
www.spenceloa.com

JSA has an equally complicated fee structure. Sending the same autograph mentioned above through JSA would cost around $40 - $20/ each autograph for a basic certification --- more for Letters of Authenticity. They require LOAs for higher-end items such as bats, guitars, uniforms, balls, etc.

Third-party authenticators are a popular way to have your items authenticated. You may even see them with booths at comic cons and signing conventions so your items can be authenticated on the spot. Whether you are in favor of third-party authenticators or not, you need to be familiar with them as you build your collection, as you will no doubt hear their names mentioned frequently.

This chapter only just touched on ways to spot obvious fakes and forgeries. One google search does not equate years of experience looking at various signatures. To prove a signature authentic or a forgery requires professional experience. But, as I have said many times already, doing your own research is a big step and a good way to start.

CHAPTER 8

IN-PERSON (IP) COLLECTING

You can also acquire celebrity autographs is the old-fashioned way: in person. Whether at the football stadium or the stage door, getting an autograph in person can range from thrilling to tedious. Let's take a look at some of the ways you can get autographs in person.

Broadway Plays

Broadway shows in New York City are a popular destination to try and snag autographs from featured performers. The most straightforward approach is waiting by the stage door after the performance has ended. After the show, you will more than likely see other people waiting, so go ahead and join the group. If you don't know where to wait, you can ask an usher or someone else affiliated with the show where the stage door is, and ask if any of the performers usually sign afterwards.

Many performers will only sign playbills from the show they are currently performing in at the theatre. For instance, if Patrick Stewart was doing his *A Christmas Carol* play, he might not sign any *Star Trek* items after the play's performance. Theoretically, this is so the celebrity can be sure they are signing for patrons who actually attended the show. However, by getting your playbill signed, you have a better chance of getting several members of the cast to sign your memento.

General guidelines for getting autographs on Broadway mostly involve common sense and are the same as any other in-person autograph hunting. Wear comfortable shoes, carry a bunch of sharpies, be polite, know people's names, and don't be too greedy. You are more likely to get an autograph if you have one item to sign, such as a playbill, rather than a stack of 20 different photos.

If you are attending a matinee show and there is another show in the evening, you may be out of luck. Many performers skip signing autographs after the matinee shows and instead will head back to their home to get some rest before the evening's performances. Do a little research and time your approach accordingly.

Movie Premieres

When most people think about obtaining celebrity autographs in person, they think of movie premieres. Celebrities getting out of their limousines, waving to the crowd, giving autographs to fans -- the images of glitz and glamour are emblazoned in our brains thanks to shows like *Extra, Entertainment Tonight*, and *TMZ*. However, the reality is that getting an autograph at a movie premiere is hard work and not guaranteed, even if you land a good spot at the barricade.

There are certain things you can do to help your chances if you do decide to try a movie premiere. First, show up early. There is such a thing as too early, however. If you arrive at the location before the metal barricades go up, you won't have any idea where to stand. Also, bringing your own chair to sit on on the sidewalk waiting for the venue to set up is a sure way to get security or the actual police to notice and ask you to move. Plan on arriving at the movie premiere three to four hours before it starts, allowing you ample time to survey the location. If it is an extremely anticipated premiere, you may want to try arriving a little earlier.

The barricade is usually set up across the street from the premiere, allowing the celebrities to exit their limousines and enter the theater without behind hounded for autographs. Once the barricades are in place, you and everybody else who arrived early will make a mad dash to grab spots in the first or second rows.

Once a celebrity makes those steps towards the barricade, expect chaos. You will be jostled and pushed as people start waving their DVDs and photos in the air, hoping to get the celebrity's attention. You may notice the person beside you suddenly has a stack of 20 photos out and ready. Yes, you guessed it -- they are a dealer. Unless you are in the first couple of rows behind the barricade, it is extremely difficult to get autographs at these events.

As I mentioned, you will be able to spot autograph dealers quickly by their stacks of photos or other items. Oftentimes security will ask them to leave or point them out to the celebrity. If a dealer does get something signed, they might then rush further down the line and try to maneuver back to the front in another spot. I am not against someone making a living, and have no real grudge against autograph dealers, but I have seen celebrities notice a dealer as being "next" in the line, then suddenly stop signing, leaving fans heartbroken and without an autograph. Once you see a true fan declined because of the actions of a dealer, it makes it harder to muster any sympathy when one of them is being escorted away.

Not every celebrity will come to the barricades to sign autographs. In fact, most probably won't. Having been on both sides of movie premieres (attending and IPing). I personally have better things to do with my day than sit out in the sun (or freeze in the cold) at a movie premiere. It is definitely a fun experience every once in awhile, but I prefer events such as comic-cons and Q&As over standing for hours upon hours, hoping a celebrity will come over to the barricade

Celebrity Q&As

If you live in the Los Angeles area, or other major cities celebrities might visit to promote their new films, there are oftentimes events where the stars will come and do a Question and Answer session (Q&A) with the audience after seeing a show or film. There are also several organizations that sponsor Q&As in the Los Angeles area, such as the Academy of Television Arts and Sciences and the Paley Center for Media.

Q&As are hit and miss for getting an autograph, even if you have a ticket to attend. I went to a Q&A with Leonardo DiCaprio for his movie *The Revenant* and he was off the stage and out the back door before the audience even had a chance to stand up and applaud. Conversely, I attended a Q&A with Logan Lerman of the *Percy Jackson* movies for

Logan Lerman giving a Q&A at a screening of his film *Indignation*. (Troy Rutter)

his film *Indignation* and he gracefully stayed, took photos, and signed autographs for anybody in attendance that wanted one.

Even if you can't attend the Q&A itself, you may be able to get an autograph by waiting outside in a traditional IP manner similar to movie premieres and Broadway shows. Be patient and courteous. There is no guarantee someone will sign, obviously, but since Q&A's are usually low-key events, the odds are a little better than at a premiere.

General Sporting Event Tips

The remainder of this chapter focuses on obtaining baseball and football autographs in person, but many of the tactics we address can be applied to other sports such as basketball, tennis, soccer, and more. The biggest tip is to wear the jersey or hat of the team in question. Even better, if you are targeting a certain player, wear their specific jersey. If you are trying to get autographs from both teams, we address that later in this chapter.

Next, bring your own items. If you have a stack of trading cards for a team, bring them. If you are doing actual footballs or baseballs, bring those as well. Purchasing items in the gift shop inside the park is expensive, and they often aren't of the best quality. If you want your baseball collection to be the same type of ball for all of your autographs, you need to bring those specific baseballs.

I would bring four items at the most to be signed by any one person. Personally, I only try to get one autograph per player, out of consideration to both the player and other fans. If you have trading cards, you can buy "photo corners" from the store and secure many cards of the same player on a piece of cardboard or on a clipboard to make it easier for a player to sign all of them quickly.

If you are bringing baseballs to sign, and want players to sign only on the "sweet spot" of the ball, *mlbsweetspot.com* offers a great accessory

Sweet Spot Jacket

called the Sweet Spot Jacket . There are many different varieties out there, but this particular one is the best I have found. You place the ball inside the jacket, revealing only the sweet spot, which almost guarantees a signature is placed right where you desire.

Sharpies are a definite must have. Bring enough in both blue and black to last the day. Sometimes a player will use your sharpie to sign other items and actually walk off with it as he goes down the line signing for other fans. You need to bring more than enough. Leave the silver and gold sharpies behind and stick with blue and black.

I also bring along some extra decoy cards (extra-thick, white cardboard blanks found in retail packs of trading cards) since they are a great way to get autographs from players you don't have merchandise

A blank autograph card for digital media celebrities. (*ttmautograph.com*)

of, or those you weren't expecting to be signing. If you don't have decoys, you might also want to invest in some blank sports-related cards such as those available from theautographcard.com or rackrs.com. These cards feature generic (or team name) designs you can use for autographs from athletes, entertainers, comic artists, and more. I even made up my own autograph card blank for YouTube, Instagram, and Internet celebrities. These are available on my website.

Also, don't forget other essentials such as sunscreen, good shoes for standing for long periods of time, snacks and a lot of patience!

Major and Minor League Baseball

During the actual baseball season, it is possible to get autographs from players before the game as they are warming up. For security reasons, it really isn't feasible any longer to try and get to players after the game, as they are getting into their cars or leaving the stadium. Get there early, as soon as the park is open to fans. Some stadiums may not allow fans to enter for practice, so do some research on the stadium before you drive to the location.

If you have never been to a particular stadium, find out which dugout each team uses. More often than not, the home team has a history of using the first-base dugout, but this isn't always the case. Knowing which dugout is in use by each team will help you plan your strategy.

Generally speaking, the best place to get autographs at baseball stadiums is along the railing in the 3-4 sections starting around first base to the outfield, and again in the same position on the third-base side. Any closer to home plate and you are behind the dugout or behind a net at home plate. Any further into the outfield and the seats are higher, making it more difficult.

Some autograph seekers will wear a generic shirt, but bring baseball caps of both teams with them. They may even bring a partner or friend who will graph one side of the field while they are graphing the other. They might switch spots the next day - or sometimes the same day - after they get items signed, switching team hats as they swap positions.

As with other celebrities, athletes are very keen on the possibility of their signatures going up on the online auction sites. Because of this, many choose to sign only for younger fans. If you are a parent or an older

Using photo corners for IP on clipboard. A wire-bound sketch book is more common.

fan, you might have a better chance of getting that prized autograph if you enlist the help of your son, daughter, younger brother or sister, or niece or nephew. The best advice is to do your research before you go to the ballpark and find out the team's official autograph policy. Then, when you are at the game a couple of hours early, be open to changes in your plan and look for opportunities.

NFL Football

The best time I have found to get autographs from NFL players is during the pre-season in the month of August. During this time, they are usually practicing and playing at venues other than their home stadium.

During NFL pre-season, the public is allowed to attend practices, and the teams also schedule specific autograph times with the players.

Many things changed in 2015, after an unfortunate incident where people were hurt during a Giants pre-season event. One of the most popular players in the game, Odell Beckham Jr., was in attendance and planned on signing. A surge of fans on one particular portion of the bleachers literally bent from fans rushing to get his autograph. According to reports, one young woman had a seizure and people walked over her to get to the front of the line. In addition, several young kids were pinned to the railing and crushed by the sheer number of people pushing forward.

Scary stuff.

In response to this, several teams implemented new autograph policies during their pre-season camps. Many teams, such as the newly relocated LA Rams, offered autograph sessions only to kids 14 and under. Even those under 14 may not receive autographs, as some teams use tokens or wristbands to keep signings to a small number. The Minnesota Vikings take things to another level. While they allow fans of all ages the chance to get autographs from most of the team, for Adrian Peterson and Teddy Bridgewater they give out 2000 scratch-off tickets. Only 150 winners will be allowed to get autographs from these star players.

Most teams arrange pre-season signing schedules based on a player's position on the roster. Running backs and wide receivers sign one day, defensive line another, and so on. For the most up-to-date schedules, check the team's official website. They all have a special section on their pre-season page detailing the exact schedule and policies for autograph sessions.

While official autograph sessions are a way to increase your chances of getting an autograph during the pre-season, you can still try at the end or beginning of practice. As with many IP situations, the goal is to arrive early and stay late. If you don't know the best places to sit for autographs, look around where people are sitting and holding signs. If in doubt, ask another fan in attendance, or even someone working at the venue. They might tell you "they have sessions later and don't sign during practice," but you can always ask further questions, such as, "If they did sign before or after practice, where is the best place?"

During the season, it gets more difficult to obtain NFL signatures both in-person at stadiums and through the mail. If you are attending an actual NFL game, the best location is around the tunnel where the players exit onto the field. You will need to get there early, and sometimes the ushers at the events will tell you a specific area is off limits without a ticket. If this happens, ask if you can just stay until the game starts. Most are accommodating, but if they say no, accept it and try to find another area. You don't want to get thrown out by security.

As with professional baseball games, if you are graphing the visiting team at a stadium, wear a hat or jersey for that team. Visiting players seem to sign more when you do. Wearing the only Vikings jersey at an Eagles vs. Vikings game in Philadelphia, for example will get you noticed. Hats are a great, easy way to "fake" being a team's fan if you are really trying to get autographs.

Some fans ask players for game-used equipment such as gloves as players are on their way through the tunnel. Some players are very generous. Personally, I stick with supplying a jersey, football, card, or some other item I actually brought to the stadium. However, I know some fans who have quite a good collection of signed, game-used memorabilia. The way you collect your autographs is up to you - do what you enjoy.

Collecting autographs at professional sporting events can be fun. Hopefully this chapter helps you devise your tactics for a successful IP graphing session. In additional to getting autographs at the sporting events, many athletes will also do personal appearances and private signings, which we will tackle next.

CHAPTER 9

COMIC CONS & PRIVATE SIGNINGS

For simplicity's sake, we will lump science fiction and comic conventions together under the term that has become well known in the fandom community: "comic-cons." The term comic-con has become a generic term used for any type of similar gathering of people around a common "geeky" interest. In this case, fantasy, science fiction, cosplay, comics, anime, and any number of other sub-genres.

Conventions come in all shapes and sizes. The most popular, San Diego Comic-Con, had over 130,000 attendees in 2016. Smaller conventions take place around the world. One such convention, OSFest in Omaha Nebraska, had only a few thousand attendees. Navigating the more popular conventions such as SDCC, Wizard World, DragonCon, or

Wondercon can be challenging, and this section gives some tips on how to get the autographs you want.

Collectors sometimes don't consider autographs acquired at these cons as "real" IP. Instead of hustling to track down your favorite celeb and get them to sign something for you, cons have celebs waiting at tables to sign. Fans are paraded by, with an assistant collecting the autograph fee. In addition to a fee for the autograph itself, there is oftentimes an additional charge for a selfie photograph with the celebrity, although many venues are now only allowing professional photograph ops costing an additional $20 or more.

Prices for autographs at conventions vary immensely not only from celebrity to celebrity, but also from year to year and even month to month. For example, I attended a convention in Chicago in 1994 and paid $20 for a photo and autograph from Mark Hamill. In 2015, his price at Celebration Europe (a popular Star Wars event) was $125. In 2016, it jumped to $174. Carrie Fisher was priced at a little over $100 for the same event. To get a multi-signed photo of the two, would be close to $300. Even so, this is a bargain at what some stores charge. At Disneyland next to Star Tours is a Mark Hamill and Carrie Fisher signed photo on sale for $1,195!

Many people have written about the prices of autographs going up over the years. Some celebs say it is because of people selling them on eBay. Others just charge based on their popularity. There are several different ways that celebs make money off attending a convention. For smaller cons, the convention might pay for plane ticket and hotel room, and the celeb gets to keep everything they make on the floor. Other conventions may provide those same conditions but also pay an appearance fee and a portion of what the celebrity brings in for photo ops.

One example of an arrangement that came into question was in 2016 at Space City Con in Galveston, Texas. According to multiple reports, the event was to feature several cast members from the TV show *Sons of*

Dual-signed Mark Hamill & Carrie Fisher on sale at Disneyland - $1,195.00!

Anarchy. There were disagreements between attending celebrities and the promoter, with both sides claiming different views of what happened. The cast members said the promoter's credit card for the hotel room and their advance checks for attending were declined. As a result, the cast didn't attend their Friday reunion panel. Fans who bought VIP tickets for the event were just out of luck. The drama unfolded across Twitter, Facebook, and other social media outlets. Even after the con, both sides continued to disagree about what occurred. While we may never have a definitive answer about what went wrong, who said what, who paid what to whom, and all the other details, it's clear that the entire situation was unfortunate for the con, the fans, and the celebrities.

When planning a trip to a convention, the best advice I can give is to plan ahead and be flexible. Look at the convention's website and examine the guest list to figure out what celebrities you are going to pay for an autograph. Be careful to note which celebrities are appearing for "Saturday only" so you can plan your time. Sometimes the websites will publish prices ahead of time. If you don't see a price for your favorite celeb's autograph, do a quick Google search such as "Nicholas Brendon autograph price" and look through the results. For instance, last year Nicholas Brendon (*Buffy the Vampire Slayer*) charged $40 for a signed photo or $30 for any item you provide.

Just because a price is published on the convention's website doesn't mean it will be that way at the con - or even the same both days. At O Comic Con in Omaha, an autograph from Jeffrey Combs was $20 one day and $30 the next, just because of an increase in demand.

Going to a convention requires money, and that means a budget. In addition to tickets, even if you live close to the area, you will need money for food, drinks, collectibles, and incidental expenses such as parking fees. These add up quickly. Make sure you come with a predefined budget. Keep in mind there are withdrawal maximums on many bank accounts. If you withdrawal $300 from an ATM Friday afternoon, you may not be able to make another withdrawal the next morning. Plan your budget and your withdrawals carefully so you have enough money to pay for your autographs in cash at the event. Most celebrities do not have credit card or "square" readers at their booths, so it is best to be prepared.

When planning your convention visit, you also have to plan your autograph signings around any guest panels you want to see. Sometimes you may want to go to a panel when your favorite celebrity is signing autographs for the last time. There isn't much I can do for you in that situation; you will have to make a choice. One of the best/worst situations

I was involved in was with Nicholas Brendon at a con in Kansas City, Missouri.

The queue line was rather long, and he was late to his table to start signing. He was scheduled for a panel with another guest in less than 30 minutes. Having waited in line for the previous hour or two, we slowly made our way to the front. I was next in line when the volunteer said, "Okay, Nicholas has to go to a panel so we are cutting the line off. You are welcome to stay in line during the panel and he will come right back." Luckily for me, the line was cut off right after me, but you can imagine how upsetting it was to everybody who had waited that long to get an autograph. They probably also wanted to go the panel he was holding, so they had to choose to wait in line and get something signed in an hour or two, or attend the panel and simply take their chances later.

Getting a signed photograph involves standing in line - a lot. It is not unusual for people to line up 2-3 hours ahead of time, just to be assured a spot in getting something signed. If you see a popular celebrity signing from 2-4 pm, you had better check out their queue at 12:30. This again is key to planning your day carefully, Leave buffer zones around your signing times. I have been to conventions where I had every intention of going to 3-4 panels and getting autographs, but at the end of the day I spent all of my time in line for just 3-4 autographs and one panel.

Many conventions open on Thursdays or Fridays. If possible, and the celebrity you are looking for will be there, I highly recommend attending these days before the weekend to get your autograph. Lines will be shorter, and you can then enjoy the weekend attending the panels. Not all conventions do this, and some celebrities will only be there from Friday-Sunday, or only on Saturday. Check the schedule and plan your itinerary. Many of the larger conventions have their own apps you can download to your phone, but in my experience these don't help much except to tell you what is going on "now" - they don't help you to plan your time with buffer zones.

Most celebs will sell you a 8x10 photograph along with the autograph. If Nichelle Nichols has an assortment of 8x10s at her table and charges $40, this includes the photograph. Some celebs will have a separate fee if you bring your own item, such as a different photo, action figure, game, or any other type of merchandise. Some will still charge you the full price. It is not uncommon for me to have a perfectly printed photograph ready with me when I go to a con, and then see the celebrity include the same one with an autograph at the booth. In these cases, I usually just buy the one they have, rather than use my own, and save my other photo for later. If you are doing out-of-the-ordinary items such as 11x17 photos, obviously you will be bringing them yourself. For these larger items, go to the local art or hobby store and look for "portfolios" that will allow you to carry your photos with you safely for the duration of the convention. They will slide into pages in the portfolio and be well protected.

When it is your turn to get an autograph, remember there are others who are waiting as well. It may help to know what you want to say, especially if you think you will "blank out" when you are face-to-face with your favorite actor or actress! Say hello, compliment them on their work, ask (and pay for) your photo, and let them know what you would like it to say. If you have an exact saying you want a celebrity to inscribe on your photo, write it on a post-it note you can put on the photo while they are signing. It makes it easier. Also, they won't (hopefully) misspell your name since it is right there on the note! This is good practice at collector shows as well.

As with IP and TTM autographs, there are people who both like and hate inscriptions on photos. In most cases, because you are buying the autographs at such a high price, there isn't much resale value. Plus, since most of the people who stand in line for a celeb's autograph are fans of the celeb (why else would you wait for 2+ hours with several hundred of your closest friends?), most fans have their autographs inscribed and personalized. It might not even be your decision. In some cases the celeb will insist on making it out to you personally. Be prepared for both cases.

The celeb may or may not let you take a picture of them signing the item. No matter what, avoid lengthy chit chat as other fans are there to meet them too. If there is a sign that says "No Selfies," you must respect that and don't ask. Finally, thank them again for being there and for signing your photo and tell them to have a nice day. Congratulations, you just got a photo from your favorite celebrity!

I always save money for 1-2 autographs ($40-50) from a celebrity who wasn't on my list but would be fun to have. Sometimes I use this fund to buy an autograph from someone who hasn't had much action at their table. When you have Peter Mayhew (Chewbacca), George Takei (Sulu), and Wil Wheaton (Wesley Crusher) at a convention, sometimes it is tough for "Gamorrean Guard from the Sail Barge in Return of the Jedi" to sell their autograph.

This practice of a "slush fund" led to one of my favorite celebrity encounters at a convention. I was waiting for a popular writer to begin signing at Phoenix Comicon, when David Franklin of Farscape came through the black curtain separating the backstage area with the convention floor. He came through the curtain with his fists pumping, shouting, "Yeah!" I looked at him and likewise went, "Yeah!" and then immediately said, "Awwwww" in disappointment. He gave a few fake boxing jabs to my arm and we laughed and he went to his booth. Later in the afternoon, I saw his table was empty so I stopped and glanced down the empty queue line until he caught my gaze and then I sighed and shrugged. He laughed. I then went over and got his autograph and we chatted for a while. At the end of the convention, I was going back to my hotel, as was he. We ended up on opposite sides of the street, crossing at the same time. As we saw each other, he just sneered in my direction and said, "Troy…" while I said, "David…" We laughed and went our separate ways. His inscription is priceless!

DAVID FRANKLIN

In addition to selfies at the table, many celebs will offer professional photo ops. These will vary in price from $40 and up. I once paid $275 for a photo op from the cast of Babylon 5 and it was worth it! But these photo ops also need to make it into your schedule. If you see a professional photo op being offered by a celeb, chances are they will not allow selfies. This is both because they want their autograph lines to move faster and they don't want to make $10 on a selfie when they will make more with the photo op.

If doing a photo op, make sure you know all of the rules. Sometimes you will have to go early to get a wristband or a ticket before your photo op. In addition, some photo ops use greenscreens so they can insert a fancy background into the photo, such as a volcanic planet or the bridge of the Enterprise. If you know a photo op is going to use a greenscreen, make sure you are not wearing a green shirt!!

There is a practice becoming standard in these types of photo ops to let people sign up for a "block" of time so you aren't waiting a long time for your photo. Do not count on this. I went to two popular conventions in the LA area, both using blocks of time for their photo ops, and they completely fell apart by not adhering to that policy. Everybody showed up at the same time and there was no enforcement - probably because the photo ops were consistently running late.

Show up early, "camera ready" (hair combed, broccoli out of teeth, etc.), and be prepared. You will be asked to put down your backpack or purse and then stand on an X and smile. Sometimes the celeb will let you strike a funny pose, but that is on a case-by-case basis. Pay attention to what those in front of you are doing and you will get a good sense of what the celeb allows. Have fun! Remember, this is the time get your photo taken with your favorite celeb, not the time to try and have a meaningful conversation. Get the photo, thank them, get your bag, and then wait for your photo to print. Be courteous to those around you and move along as quickly as you can while still having fun. Sometimes you will also get a business card with a special website URL on it so you can download a digital version of the photo.

The author and John Hurt at a professional photo-op. (Troy Rutter)

At a smaller convention, it is likely you will see your favorite celebs in the halls as they make their way to a panel, signing, photo op, or back to their hotel room. You may also see them eating dinner at the hotel restaurant. Resist the urge to stop them to ask for an additional autograph or selfie while they are out and about. Chances are, they are trying to make their way to their next event, and getting stopped will make them late, setting the schedule back later and later. If they are going back to their hotel room or going out to eat, they are just finishing an exhausting day of signing autographs and being on panels. I know that after a day at a convention, I am exhausted just by being around so many people and meeting my favorite celebs - can you imagine how tired a celebrity will be from signing, doing panels, and basically performing all day? Give them some space and privacy. A simple "hello" and a smile is enough. Don't follow them to their room or take photos of them eating.

Finally, some convention basics. First, wear comfortable shoes. If you are cosplaying, this can be difficult, so it may be worth trying to get your autographs on a day where you aren't in costume. This isn't to say the celebs don't enjoy seeing you get an autograph wearing a costume from the series or movie they were on - they do! It is purely a matter of personal preference and being comfortable. Be sure to drink plenty of water, and do not rely on soda, energy drinks, and alcohol. Most discomfort at conventions can be attributed to uncomfortable shoes and lack of hydration, so those two are a must. You may also want to pack several snacks so you can keep your energy up when standing in long lines. I am a big fan of Justin's Almond Butter packets: they are squeezable almond butter packets that are easy to carry and disposable.

There are also some supplies you can have on hand to make sure your autograph session goes as smoothly as possible. First, you might bring along your own silver, gold, or other colored sharpie to use on your photo. Sharpies dry out often at signings, and the last thing you want is a signature that is barely legible due to using a bad, dried-out marker. I always take an arrangement of silver, gold, blue, and black with me, just in case I see theirs is running low on ink. Another item I take are 8x10 top loaders. These are hard, transparent cards photos slide into to protect them. You can also use standard sheet protectors. But be careful! Both top loaders and sheet protectors can smear the autograph if it isn't dry. So let the autograph dry for several minutes before you put them into a protective sleeve. Most experts say to avoid keeping autographs in 8x10 top loaders for extended periods of time, as they tend to stick to the plastic. I prefer Ultra Pro clear pocket protectors with acid-free backing boards to keep my autographs safe. It is best to buy these supplies before the convention, because if any booths are selling them, you will be paying a premium.

Comic-cons are a great way to meet your favorite celebrities and other fans. By planning your day and having a plan of attack, you can make sure it is both fun and that you get to see everything you would like to. I hope this chapter provided some new tips for you to try on your next convention outing. Good luck!

Private Signings

Private signings are events where you can either pre-order a certain photograph or send in one of your own items for a celebrity to autograph on a specific date. The public is not allowed to attend, hence the term "private signing." Private signings have had some controversies over the years, oftentimes due to higher than normal prices.

In 2015, fans noticed many items being returned from Gene Wilder, star of the popular *Willy Wonka & The Chocolate Factory* film, appeared to be done with a stamp and not personally signed. Later, a notice went out that Gene wasn't signing autographs through the mail any longer. Shortly after that, a private signing was announced. The price for an authentic signed photo was now listed at $199. Fans were outraged, both at their returned collectibles getting a fake stamp and at the inflated price.

It is often thought that private signings are done by celebrities who don't sign through the mail very often, or who refuse to sign most things in person. While this has some truth to it, not every celebrity who holds a private signing has given up on signing through the mail. Oftentimes a private signing event is agreed to by a celebrity because they are too busy to go to cons or other personal appearances.

Another controversy erupted in 2016 when it was announced that Daisy Ridley from *Star Wars: The Force Awakens* would be doing a private signing for $300-$600 per autograph, which more than doubled what many of the original *Star Wars* actors were charging. Many fans were suspicious, and even Daisy was confused. Fans went into an uproar, claiming it was a scam, but eventually the signing took place and items were authenticated by PSA/DNA as they were signed. The entire controversy appeared to be a misunderstanding, but that didn't help fans' perceptions of private signings. Many are still perplexed as to why Daisy's autograph costs more than an original *Star Wars* cast autograph.

Some private signings are streamed live over the Internet, with the celebrity talking to the camera as they are signing. One such infamous signing involved William Shatner. When Shatner got to a particularly long inscription for known autograph collector Zane Savage, he refused to write what he was supposed to and protested in front of the camera, simply signing his name to the photo.

William Shatner during a private signing streamed live. (Zane Savage)

Private signings are usually announced via a celebrity's social media channels or website, or on the site of a promoter. These announcements are then shared on many of the forums around the Internet. There is usually a start date for when "tickets" go on sale. Again, these are not tickets to attend the event in person. You are given instructions on how to send your item in to be signed, or asked to pick a photo after buying your ticket. You can include a short inscription if you want one as well. You then send in your items to be signed, follow the given instructions, and then wait for the signing to take place and for your item to be shipped back to you.

Many private signings have third-party authenticators on site during the signing and will include the price of authentication, including certificate, in the autograph price. Sometimes having the item authenticated involves an optional fee.

PSA/DNA Booth at a convention offering to authenticate autographs (Troy Rutter)

An alternative to private signings is to buy an autograph through the celebrity's website if they offer them. One great example of this is the Fourth Doctor, Tom Baker of *Doctor Who*. On his website, you can choose a photograph, get it autographed, and choose from some pre-written inscriptions or provide your own. The autograph is then mailed to you quickly. Mine came back in less than a week!

Other celebrities may sign autographs in bulk and give them to their manager or friend who handles their website so they can handle the shipping process, and not have to deal with inscriptions. These are still real autographs, and many people prefer them without inscriptions anyway, so they are still a good value, especially if the celebrity doesn't usually sign through the mail.

Tom Baker signed photo purchased through his website (Troy Rutter)

CHAPTER 10

BUYING AUTOGRAPHS

I have to admit, this is a hard chapter to write. Not because it's something I am unfamiliar with, but because sometimes the truth hurts. Whenever you talk about buying autographs, it means someone else is selling. And whenever there is a monetary transaction, battle lines are drawn quickly and people on both sides of the relationship start trash talking the other. It happens.

Auction Sites and Amazon

The most popular place for buying and selling of autographs is eBay. I put this chapter after "real or fake" for a reason. Many of the concerns and warning signs mentioned in that chapter apply to buying autographs as well. Amazon is much like eBay in the way items are offered, which is why I include them together in this chapter.

I am not a big fan of buying autographs. Because the actual value of an autograph will almost never go up in this day and age (my opinion), I personally prefer obtaining an autograph in person or through the mail. But if you have that one card in your set that is missing, or there is one celebrity you are trying desperately to get, then purchasing the autograph may be your best bet.

The big thing to remember when buying an autograph is that Certificates of Authenticity (COAs) are not worth the paper they are printed on. I can sign a photo of Ringo Starr and print my own COA in full color stating the autograph is real.

Proof that anybody can create a COA. (Troy Rutter)

I once knew of someone who sold costumes "from" a popular TV show, complete with a wardrobe tag and COA, when all he really had was a color printer and a self-inking stamp of the show's logo, plus a supply of blank wardrobe tags. COAs only make an auction listing sound reputable to the untrained collector. When buying an autograph, don't be afraid of auctions that do not have a COA, and likewise don't automatically assume an autograph is authentic if it has one. As with so many things, do your research on any autograph you are considering purchasing.

If you are looking for baseball card autographs, there are a wide variety of different things you can look for. The market is saturated with various kinds of autographed baseball cards. There are cards signed TTM, patch cards, bat cards, numbered cards, parallels, on-card, stickers, relics, and more. If you are looking for a certified on-card autograph, you will have it a little easier, as these are hard to fake. If you are buying a standard trading card with nothing more than a signature on it, you really need to do your research to verify its authenticity.

Sometimes you can find some good deals by searching eBay for certain keywords or phrases. For instance, searching for "autograph card lot" will turn up auctions containing more than one autograph in a single auction. You can vary your keywords to drill down to a specific card you are looking for. "JJ Watt patch autograph numbered" will find all numbered patch autographs for the popular football player.

Look closely at the detailed description once you find an autograph you may be interested in. Again, don't let any mention or omission of a COA influence your decision. Read the description carefully and if it says reprint or preprint, pass on the purchase. Do a Google image search for the player's in-person autograph and compare it to the photo in the auction. Do they look similar? Make sure you are comparing a signature known to be authentic, such as a certified on-card autograph, and not another photo from the same seller or TTM if you can help it. If everything still looks good, it is finally up to you whether or not the autograph is worth it and whether you will place a bid or even "buy it now."

What are autographs worth? Whatever someone will pay for them. I have seen some recent football cards that look great go up on eBay from a reputable source for thousands of dollars. Would I buy a modern football card for that much? No. Would I buy any baseball or football card for that much? Probably not, but that's just me. Dealers and sellers will sell their items at any price they think they will make the most profit. You can usually get a good feel of a celebrity's autograph price by looking at similar auctions.

It is worth mentioning that when you are searching for an autograph on eBay, you are seeing the price that the seller wants to sell it for, not what others have actually bought it for in the past. A trick I do when pricing autographs is to look for a similar item and see what it actually sold for. My process is pretty simple. First I find an autograph I am interested in. Then I open up a new tab in my web browser and go to eBay again. This time I click on Advanced Search and select the checkbox next to "Completed Auctions" and another checkbox next to "Sold" and perform the same search again. This shows what the same card sold for in previous auctions. I regularly see popular cards on eBay with a starting price of thousands of dollars, then search completed auctions to find they actually sold for far less. If you do this research, you may be able to make an offer to the seller, or just wait for someone else to list the item at a more reasonable price.

Signed photos and posters are different than certified trading cards. When looking to buy a signed photo from a celebrity, you need to do all the same research I covered previously. Something to consider is that you are not only buying the photo and autograph, but you are also paying for the convenience of not standing on the corner by a celeb's hotel yourself. Part of the price of a purchased autograph includes the "business" of buying from an autograph dealer. You are paying for their time and effort in obtaining the autograph.

As with COAs, a photo of a celeb signing the item is worthless. It is very easy to get one item signed, take a photo of the celeb signing the item, and then simply make 100 more fake ones, each accompanied by the same photo of the item being signed. These types of photos are oftentimes noted in the description as "photo proof," and while it may add to the odds of an item being legitimate, you still need to do your research.

Bottom line: do not treat COAs and photo proof as a definitive indication of an item's authenticity.

Check Out My Cards - COMC.com

COMC.com is a popular website for both buying and selling autographs. If you sell cards via the site, you receive credit so you can purchase other ones from their inventory. Buying cards from *comc.com* is as simple as using a standard shopping cart on any website. Add to your cart, check out, pay, and wait for it to be shipped to you. They are a good place to get cards at the going price since most of their prices are normalized across all people selling the same card.

Thrift Stores, Estate Sales and Garage Sales

Thrift stores, estate sales, and garage sales can all provide both a welcome surprise and a big headache. Unlike with auction sites and being in front of your computer, it is difficult to judge the authenticity of an item when trying to compare signatures on your smartphone. While there are stories of finding valuable autographs in the bottom of a bin at a thrift store, this doesn't happen very often.

One item many people have found in good supply at thrift stores are signed books. Once you begin looking, you will get a feel as to what books have the possibility of being signed. It is hit and miss, and some people spend a good amount of time trying to find signatures with no success. Good books to check for autographs include those by politicians and local authors, as well as biographies. Books of any topic can be signed, however, so if you have the time to spend looking through the shelves, you might find a good deal!

Another item you can find at thrift stores are collections of cards, or even full sets. Many card companies will liquidate or even just donate box sets of old cards to charities such as Salvation Army or Goodwill. Or a collector may be moving and decide to donate their collection and be done with them. It never hurts to ask someone working at the store if they have any baseball or football cards available.

Estate sales are a little easier in terms of taking a chance and evaluating whether something is real or not. For instance, if you go to an estate sale and there is a good number of items from a certain sports team in a "man cave," the chances of those items being legitimate may be better than those at a thrift store. If you look around at other items for sale and it looks like they are/were a collector, you can feel a little better about the items' likely authenticity. If there is an entire wall of signed magazine covers of politicians and the person was active in politics, I would wager those magazines were signed in person.

Relics and Pack Searching

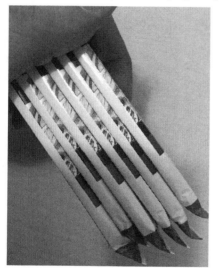
Looking for relics by thickness. (Troy Rutter)

The popularity of autographs, particularly in baseball and football card packs, has led trading card companies such as Topps, Panini, and others to feature signed cards and "relics" as random inserts in card packs. Next time you go to a major department store, take a glance at the trading card aisle (now populated with card games like Yu-Gi-Oh!, Pokemon, Magic: The Gathering, and others) and look for people with stacks of card packs in their hands. If they are standing there for a long time, chances are you are witnessing one of the troubling side-effects of these random relic inserts: pack searching.

By carefully looking at and feeling the packs, it is possible to guess which of the packs contain a "hit" -- i.e., a patch card, relic, or autographed card -- with a pretty good success rate. The simplest of these techniques is to look at the thickness of the packs in comparison with others. Card companies quickly caught on to pack searchers and started including decoys, thick blank cards, to try and throw pack searchers off.

A popular pack searching technique is called swiping. You run your fingers over the front of the pack and try to feel for a raised area (if it is a sticker autograph) or for other unusual variations in the pack thickness that might be a tip-off that a patch or relic might be enclosed. Another easy one is a bend test, where you gently flex the packs. If the pack doesn't bend, you might have a patch or other relic.

Pack searching remains prevalent in the large department stores but usually is not tolerated in card stores. Please note, I am not trying to encourage pack searching, just giving a brief overview of the process and a description of what pack searching is. For some funny examples of people caught pack searching, go to YouTube and search for "pack searcher." Watch just how ridiculous grown adults look when trying to get an autograph or relic card from a pack in the store.

I have seen kids at hobby stores opening packs of both sports and other cards near a trash can, literally opening and throwing the common cards directly into the trash and keeping the hits. This is extreme but it does happen. Personally, I have stopped buying cards at the big-box stores, and avoid individual packs altogether. If you buy a hobby box, most guarantee one or more autographs or relics per box. That is significantly better odds than getting an autograph in the wild from an overly searched store such as Target or Walmart.

Pack searchers often go store to store, especially in larger cities where there are more of the big-name stores in close proximity. If you look on YouTube, you will find some people who make a whole weekend out of it, searching their state for hot packs. While some try and hide it, others are proud of it. Oftentimes the found pack itself will be listed on eBay without being opened. This is called a "hot pack" because the unknown contents of a hot pack are considered more valuable than an unpopular autograph from a relatively unknown player. The price pack searchers receive on eBay for found cards is seen as profitable, so the practice will continue and evolve as the card companies try to thwart their efforts.

The hobby is divided between those who think pack searching is okay and those who don't. Pack searchers think collectors who don't search packs are wasting their money on worthless packs, and those who don't like pack searching think pack searches are ruining the hobby. I try to avoid the issue altogether by only buying hobby boxes. Next time you see someone in the card aisle, bending the packs or running their finger across the tops, now you know why. It is up to you if you want to alert the store manager or not, but if you do, they will just be back later.

Convention Dealers

At any comic-con or media convention, you are bound to see an autograph dealer in the dealer room or expo hall. These dealers commonly sell already-signed photos of a variety of celebrities, and sometimes even those attending the convention. These autographs are usually obtained over the years as the dealer visits different conventions or bought from other dealers who get items in person. As far as authenticity goes, in my experience these dealers tend to offer authentic signatures, but you still need to do your due diligence.

One common scenario is if you are attending a big *Doctor Who* convention with two actors who portrayed the Doctor, and a dealer is selling other Doctor Who autographs. In my opinion, these dealers can be trusted more than, say, an estate sale or eBay. In addition, many of these dealers will sell autographs that are already certified by PSA/DNA or some other authenticator. Again, this is not a guarantee of authenticity, but it does help the odds.

Buying from convention dealers is pretty straightforward, and most have a credit card reader available at the table. Sometimes the dealer may sell an autograph of a celebrity attending the show for more than the celebrity is charging just a few feet away. This is perfectly normal since at a busy convention you have to pick and choose your schedule, and it may work out better to buy it from a dealer and not waste an hour or two of your time. You pay for the service and convenience of not having to wait in line. Of course, you won't be meeting the celebrity in person, but it is a good fallback if your schedule doesn't work out.

Personally, I tend not to buy autographs in the dealer's room very often unless it is spur-of-the-moment and a good deal. You can also sometimes find supplies such as 8x10 top loaders and sheet protectors if you forgot yours at home. They may also have better or more unique unsigned photos of the celebrities available that may be worth the $5 extra to have handy.

Many dealers will tell you they are members of one organization or another. This shouldn't be a major factor in judging the legitimacy of an autograph. Anybody can create their own association. Two of the largest organizations for autograph dealers are the Professional Autograph Dealers Association (PADA) and the Universal Autograph Collector's Club (UACC). Both of these organizations were formed to help self-police the industry and recognize dealers who are legitimate, fair, and not selling replicas or fakes. Both PADA and UACC are good organizations, but a dealer claiming to be a member is not reason to take a dealer's claims of authenticity at face value.

Comic Book and Memorabilia Stores

You can find stores selling signed merchandise almost everywhere. Keep in mind that just because a store may be in the middle of Kearney, Nebraska - do not assume the memorabilia being sold is authentic. As I have said before, always do your research.

A variety of autographs being sold at Universal Citywalk. (Troy Rutter)

Celebrities vs Autograph Dealers

Celebrities like Mark Hamill and others routinely criticize dealers for being unethical. This has led to many celebrities saying they won't sign autographs at all because they are afraid it will end up eBay in a matter of hours. While it is true that many autographs end up on popular auction sites, it is fairly easy to spot a dealer in a crowd when you are graphing IP. They show up with 5, 10, or more photos and are there to try and get as many photos as they can signed by the celebrity. Contrast that with someone else at the same location, just trying to get one photo they printed out themselves at home. As I wrote about in the chapter on IP autographs, some IP hunting attempts can get pretty intense.

One of the questions many people have is if autograph dealers are the reason prices of autographs at conventions have risen over the years. I personally think it is part of the equation, but not for the reasons most consider. Many think because autographs are being sold on eBay, a celebrity will raise their price at a convention to try and combat those who are selling and make the return on investment less for the dealers. Unfortunately, this punishes the average fan who just wants a photo of their favorite celebrity.

Consider someone selling a celebrity's autograph on an auction site for $30, while the celebrity is charging $40 or more at a convention. By the sheer nature of competition, people may be more willing to buy the autograph at $30 than spend the $40 or more at the convention. So, because they are physically selling fewer photos, they need to get a better return on investment. So they raise their prices to $50 or $60. This kind of reciprocal relationship with dealers is common, and unfortunately, some celebrities have stopped signing altogether, or opt only for private signings with higher-than-average costs.

At the end of the day, an autograph is only worth what people will pay for it. I believe that 80% or more of autographs obtained through the mail or IP are kept by their original owners because they have a vested interest in the celebrity. Dealers and sellers make up a small percentage of autograph seekers. Sure, people will sell a photo for many different reasons, but my personal opinion is that celebrities should embrace fans and the autograph industry. In time, the value of their signature may go down, but if a celeb is relying solely on proceeds from autograph signings to make ends meet, there are other issues they should be worried about. Again, just my personal opinion.

Autograph dealers are trying to make a living in a volatile marketplace. There are good and bad dealers, just like there are good and bad teachers, religious leaders, or members of any other profession. As always, you need to do your research if you are thinking of buying from an autograph dealer. Discount any mention of COA, photo proof, or belonging to any dealer association. Look at the autograph you are interested in buying and compare it to others. Doing research will greatly increase your chances at an authentic autograph at a great price.

CHAPTER 11

STORAGE AND DISPLAY

When those autographs start arriving in your mailbox, you are going to need a way to store them. Fortunately, the most common storage options can be found in most every department store, such as Walmart or Target. But as your collection grows, you will want to take a more organized approach to storing them. After all, you waited a long time for some of those sends to come back, so you want to make sure they are all protected but easy to show and share, right?

Trading and Sports Cards

Whether you display your autographs on a wall, shelf, or in a binder, you can make sure your collection remains a source of pride by using the correct storage methods. Whether it is a simple baseball card or a signed, slightly deflated football from the Super Bowl, properly storing and displaying your autographs is definitely something to consider.

<u>Penny Sleeves</u>

I tried searching the Internet to learn exactly why these little pieces of plastic are called "penny sleeves," but all I came up with is that they literally cost a penny or less. If there is a big history of the penny sleeve somewhere that I'm missing, I'm sure people will let me know.

Penny sleeves are thin, plastic card protectors you can use for a lot of things. The main use for penny sleeves is to create a barrier between the card and whatever storage medium you are using to hold the card. For instance, if you are using nine--pocket pages for your trading cards, you can buy snug-fitting penny sleeves to put encase the card before putting them into the pockets. This helps protect the card from abrasion. The same holds true for any other type of storage, including top loaders, mag cases, grading cases, etc. The penny sleeve provides one more layer of protection against the card being scratched. They are cheap, so use them.

<u>Top Loaders</u>

Top loaders are thicker, single-pocket pieces of plastic that are used to hold a card or other flat items such as a photo. They vary from trading card size up through 8x10 and larger, as well as by width to accommodate thicker cards such as relic and patch cards. The width of toploaders are measured in points. The most common top loaders are standard sports-card size and thickness of 20 points. If you have thicker cards and you don't know what size top loader to get, please use the guide beginning on the following page.

- 1 Regular Card = 20 Points. Use standard or regular-size top loaders.
- 3 Regular Cards = 55 Points. Use 55-point top loaders. These may also be called Action Packed Size or Thick)
- 4-5 Regular Cards = 70-75 Points. Use 75-point top loaders or Extra Thick Holders
- 6-8 Regular Cards = 120-130 Points. Use 130-point top loaders, often called Memorabilia or Real Thick.
- 9-12 Regular Cards = 180 Points. Use 180-point top loaders, also called Super Thick.

Top loaders should always be used with a penny sleeve. You will find some collectors on forums who say they aren't necessary, but since they are so cheap, why take the risk? Slip on a penny sleeve and then carefully put them into the top loader. Be careful not to use the card corners to "open" the top loader or you might damage the card.

Even standard top loaders come in a variety of styles. You will see top loaders emblazoned with "Rookie Card," "Top Prospect," or even "Hall of Fame." Personally, I don't purchase top loaders with writing on them, as they tend to be different sizes and will not fit in my standard trading card boxes for storage. Stick with regular-size top loaders, especially Ultra Pro, and you won't go wrong. Speaking of Ultra Pro, they are by far the superior manufacturer of plastic storage alternatives for all of your collectibles. With the exception of their binders, Ultra Pro just can't be beat.

If you are organizing your cards by team, you can also find a variety of hard acrylic cases that will hold 10, 20, 100, or more cards. These are great for sorting your cards. The downside to these hard acrylic cases is, while they will fit cards with penny sleeves, you can't fit top loaders inside them. I tend to use the acrylic cases for cards I am waiting to buy top loaders for, or for cards of a particular team or set I want to keep separate from the others.

Pocket Pages

For sports cards, the most common storage medium is the nine-pocket sheet protector. These are clear pieces of plastic that hold nine sports cards on a single page. Quality is important when it comes to pocket pages. While you might get a deal for a "starter pack" of an off-brand at Walmart, there is a noticeable difference when you move up to a higher quality brand of pockets. The best quality I have found for the past 20+ years are Ultra Pro. Ultra Pro makes some of the best storage options for sports cards (and other collectibles) out there. Their plastic is thick, crystal clear, and helps keep cards from fading. In addition, and this is important, the openings on the card pages stay closed and do not let the cards fall out if the binder is accidentally rotated upside -down. This is very important! With many of the cheaper brands of pocket pages, the cards can fall out very easily. Nobody wants to leave a trail of autographed baseball cards in their wake just because they accidentally flipped the binder upside down! One hundred pages of Ultra Pro pockets will run you about $20 - storing some 900 cards for $20. While it is possible to store 18 cards per page (front and back), I personally like sticking to one card per pocket.

If you want pocket pages that are a little less expensive, you can try another good brand, BCW. BCW is in the middle- to high-quality range when it comes to sports card protectors. Some say they even rate up there with Ultra Pro. BCW brand pocket pages will run about $15 for 100 pages.

The worst value are Staples and Avery brand card pages (available near the report covers at Walmart or Target), or pages from Hobby Lobby and Michaels. The Staples brand has the unfortunate characteristic of letting cards fall out of the pockets. Stick with the best. You can find smaller packages of Ultra Pro pages in the card aisle at Walmart and Target, so they are easily available.

<u>Binders</u>

Trading card binders come in a variety of shapes and sizes. Some are padded and oversized, while some have the words "Baseball Cards" or "Collector's Album" embossed in gold on the front and the spine. If you read the reviews of dedicated sports card binders on the Internet, you will find people who both love and hate specialized binders. Thanks to the popularity of collecting, you can find binders that say "Magic: The Gathering," "Football Cards," "Baseball Cards," "Pokemon," and just about anything else. In the end, though, a binder is a binder, and what you need it to do is hold card pages in a sturdy way.

The important thing to look for in a binder are the rings. Standard binder rings for 1-2" binders are round rings that open and close by pulling them apart. The best binders have the best rings. I have purchased numerous binders where one day the rings just won't close. At this point in a binder's lifespan, the pages start falling out, or they become misguided when you flip through them. It then becomes a real hassle to look through your collection, or to add additional pages.

Unless you are planning to have a pretty bookcase full of binders that say "Collector's Album," save your money and don't buy specialized binders, even if they come from a trusted name like Ultra Pro. One of the common defects of these padded binders is that, even after minimal use, the padded covers begin to tear, revealing the underlying cardboard. Whether this is due to actual misuse, or the plastic shrinking over time, I am not sure. But it happens - a lot.

Go to your favorite office supply store and find the section with binders and you will be presented with many options. My personal favorites are 3" heavy-duty binders, with or without the insertable covers and spines. These binders usually have "D" rings (the shape of the rings that hold the pages), and some even have a little device that helps lock the rings closed. You can choose any color you want, but I prefer black, as it just looks sharp on the shelf. Because binders are constantly being improved and styles changed, you may want to buy 2-3 of the same kind to have on hand. Pro-tip: Keep the packaging showing the specific brand of binder for your files, or make a note of it somewhere so you can get the same one again later. A 3" binder could technically hold 100 pages, but 50 would be a good number before it starts to be cumbersome to insert new pages.

Another option, if you want something a little more "showy," is photo albums. You can find photo albums that accept regular-size card pocket pages in just about every department store. Cheap photo albums, however, will have the same failings as I mentioned above, with the plastic ripping. Some of the best photo albums I have found are at Hobby Lobby. Just be sure to get the pocket pages someplace else! I again recommend getting more than one album at a time, and keeping the packaging (or taking a photo with your cell phone camera). I can't tell you how many times I have gone back to the store only to be unable to find the album I purchased, or unable to remember the exact kind.

Monster Boxes

Graduating from a shoe box or a plastic box to a monster box is a rite of passage. A typical monster box for trading cards has several rows that securely hold thousands of baseball cards. By far the best boxes I have ever used come from BCW. They have small boxes and very large boxes. One of their bigger boxes is a five-row monster box capable of holding 5,000 cards (slightly less when using top loaders). I have several of these boxes and sort them into teams, as well as signed and unsigned. For instance, I have one monster box full of unsigned baseball cards sorted by team, and another monster box of signed baseball cards sorted by player. Same for football. As your collection grows, you can always add more boxes to expand and organize your collection.

Monster boxes are a great way to store your cards in top loaders, as well as your common cards. If you get smaller, one-row boxes, chances are your top loader cards won't fit. These one-row boxes are made for the cards to lie down on their long side, not the short edge. Thus, with top loaders, they end up being "too long" and won't fit in the box. You won't have this problem with multi-row monster boxes. I use several sizes of monster boxes that range from two rows all the way up to 5 rows for cards

Standard 5 row monster box sold by BCW. (Troy Rutter)

You can buy plastic dividers to separate different teams and sports. Because the dividers are shorter than top loaders, they work best with cards not in top loaders. If you need a divider between top loaders, use a decoy card in front of the plastic dividers.

Photos and Other Memorabilia

Sheet Protectors

If you collect 8x10 photos, 11x14 photos, postcards, or any other paper-weight memorabilia, you can usually find a product from Ultra Pro for storing your items. For photos, look for one-pocket sheet protectors that come in either 8 1/2 x 11 sizes from Ultra Pro, or 8x10 sizes from BCW. Pair these with an acid-free magazine backing board for extra protection. You can also buy pocket pages that fit a variety of other sizes. Do a search on amazon.com for Ultra Pro, or visit your local card shop. They will have a variety of different pocket pages available.

<u>Acrylic Cases</u>

Acrylic cases for larger items are best ordered online, as many hobby stores don't carry the entire line of cases. You can find acrylic cases sized for footballs, baseballs, basketballs, baseball bats, and other items. For

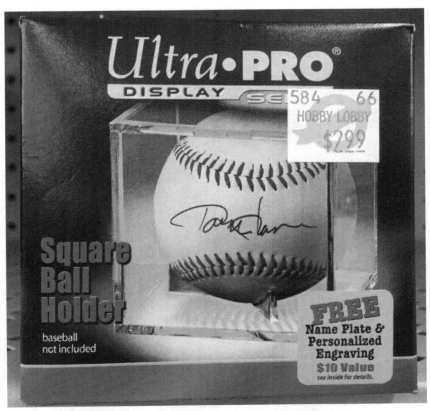

Some acrylic storage boxes can be found at hobby stores. (Troy Rutter)

baseballs, I highly recommend going with a square acrylic protector rather than a round holder with a base. Not only is the plastic on these holders sometimes cheaply made, but because it is round, you can't stack multiple baseballs on top of each other without a shelf. Buying a square acrylic case specifically made for baseballs is definitely the way to go, and you can usually buy a small case of them cheaper than you can individually.

Backer Boards

If you are familiar with collecting comic books and magazines, you are probably already familiar with backer boards. For comics, you generally buy a plastic bag to store the comic books in and then slip in an acid-free backer board to help protect it from bending. The same type of board can be used for storing autographed photos. This is one of the main reasons I like the Ultra Pro full-page protectors rather than the BCW 8x10 protectors. Magazine backing boards are in the standard magazine/letter size of 8 1/2 x 11, which fit perfectly into standard one-pocket pages. If you instead purchase 8x10 specific pocket pages, you will have to trim off the sides and top of the backer board to fit into the page. This is a big chore.

Playbills

They make binders and pages that fit playbills too! You don't need a fancy playbill binder, just look for a 5 3/8" by 8 1/2" binder at your office supply store. They will have some pocket pages for it as well, but if they do not, look on *amazon.com* or go to my website at *ttmautograph.com* for a link to my personal favorite binders and pages.

Frames

If you watch my YouTube videos, you will see I display some of my autographed photos taped to the wall in the background without frames. This is "movie magic" - do not do this! What I don't show in the videos is that the ones on the wall are actually copies of the originals, which are stored neatly in Ultra Pro protectors and backing boards in binders on my shelf. When I first started collecting autographs, I would put them in cheap frames and place them on the wall around the border of my room. Over the years, I started noticing the white paper in my very first autograph slowly becoming discolored. Photographs age with time, and being in direct sunlight will only increase that aging process.

Unfortunately, not many of us can afford true museum-quality framing products. If you really want to display your photos on your wall, use a quality frame. You can buy 8x10 photo frames with UV protection, which filters out 98% of UV rays, online for about $8 each. While more expensive than the $2 frames you can buy at Walmart or Target, they will help protect your autographs for many years to come. If you simply must use cheap frames, the best advice I can give is to make sure the autograph isn't in direct sunlight (directly opposite a window, for instance) and in a fairly constant temperature. I would not recommend putting any autographs you care about on the front porch, for instance, especially in the midwest, as temperature and humidity changes can severely ruin your photo.

Posters are best professionally framed rather than using the ready-made frames at retail stores. The extra money spent framing a multi-signed poster is well worth it.

You might be overwhelmed with all the storage options available for trading cards. Most people are familiar with only the standard-size protectors, but as you have read, there are so many more options out there. In addition to what I have listed, you can also find screw-down cases, magnetic cases (same as a screw-down, but using magnets), four screw-downs per case, and many other storage and display options. Take a trip to your local card store and see what they have, and if you have questions - ask them! They are more than happy to help someone just starting in the hobby, especially if you will be a repeat customer!

Don't be afraid to display your autograph collection - you have worked hard for it! But be responsible and take care when storing and displaying them. A little common sense goes a long way.

CHAPTER 12

SOCIAL SHARING

It used to be, in order to share your collection with friends, you had to invite them over to see your autographs on display . You grabbed a binder or two of autographs from under the coffee table and watched your friends' reactions as they leafed through the autographs. These days, it is possible to share your collection with the world thanks to the Internet and social media networks such as Facebook, YouTube, Instagram, Snapchat, and more.

You don't need any fancy cameras or expensive lighting to get started sharing your autographs. If you have a camera on your cell phone, it can take great photos of your autographs. You can email them to yourself to post on your social media accounts or you can post directly from your phone. Using social media is a fun way to share your collection and make new friends. I have been creating YouTube videos for my "mail days" for years and have made friends all over the world. Over time, you might do mutual giveaways and contests to help break up the monotony of the hobby and rejuvenate your excitement for collecting.

Unfortunately, a book really isn't the best way to teach you everything I know about all of the different social media outlets and how to produce content others will engage with. Instead, I will try and give you some introductory material for each of the major social media networks so you can get started and gradually increase your knowledge on how to produce content for each individual service.

YouTube

YouTube is at the forefront of the TTM community. In addition to autograph collecting, the YouTube community dealing strictly with baseball cards is very active. To find other collectors, all you have to do is search YouTube for "TTM" or "autograph" and you will find hundreds of

Front page of my YouTube Channel. (Troy Rutter)

community members uploading videos to their channels.

The quality of videos varies from creator to creator, but you don't have to use a fancy camera if you don't have one. One collector who was very active from 2012-2013 never showed their face. They used a fishbowl as the background on their videos instead. Videos can be as intricate as you like, with zooms and captions, or you can keep it simple. The important thing is that you are sharing your collection and your returns with the rest of the community.

If you want to invest in a good setup, here are some tips. While a cell phone can take very good videos and photos, most "big" YouTubers use a DSLR camera such as a Canon T6i. These cameras were originally designed to take still photos, but ever since the Canon T2i, they have been used for video and are a popular choice for vloggers (video bloggers). A good tripod is also recommended if using a DSLR. Lighting is also important. I admit I go a little overboard when it comes to lighting and production quality, but it is important that people can actually see the autographs you are showing. There is nothing worse than knowing someone received a really great autograph in the mail but you can't see it because it is too dark, there's too much glare, or the video is shaky.

Another important part of being a part of any community is interacting with others. On YouTube, as well as the other social media services, this is done by commenting on videos or photos, giving them a "like" or "favoriting," and also subscribing to social media streams. When you subscribe to someone's channel or feed, you receive a notification when the creator you subscribed to posts content you might be interested in.

I spend a lot of time editing my photos with cutaways and zooms, as well as a custom intro that plays before the video, but many of the most popular TTM videos are from collectors who start their video at the beginning and then hit stop at the end, without editing at all. Again, it is not necessary to have thousands of dollars' worth of equipment in order to join any of these communities. Start an account, upload a video, and start engaging with other people. Everybody has to start somewhere!

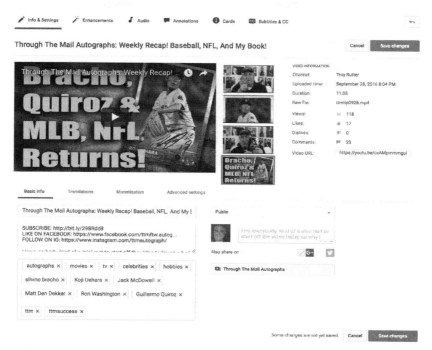

Editing the description, tags and thumbnail of a video. (Troy Rutter)

After uploading your video, there are a few of things you can do to make sure your video stands out. First, you can upload a custom thumbnail serving as your video's preview before it plays. Take a picture of an autograph in your video. After you create a free account on canva.com, there is a template called YouTube Thumbnail you can select and then upload your photos and add text. It is a great way to save time, especially if you do not own a professional graphics program like Photoshop.

The next thing you want to do is be sure you fill out the "tags" portion of your video's description. Once you start typing in the tags area, it will autocomplete with a suggested tag. My tagging area has not worked for the last year or so due to an unknown bug with YouTube, so I just type the keywords or tags into the box. Using these tags will help YouTube display your thumbnail among other related videos for people browsing the service.

There are tons of other tips on creating YouTube videos that are not practical to discuss in this book. I have attended numerous conferences and watched endless videos about optimizing YouTube channels, creating playlists, etc. Once you get started, it is important you do it for the fun of it or you will quickly burn out. There have been many creators over the years who decided to get "gung ho" and do as many videos as they could, only to suffer burnout and let their channel decay. While burnout is something we all deal with from time to time, it is important to stay positive. If, however, you really don't feel like doing videos any longer, go ahead and take a break. Your channel may take a subscriber hit without any new content, but in the end you are more important than likes, views, or subscribers. Your audience will understand if you need a break -- it happens to everyone.

Once you have uploaded your video, let people know about it! Use your other social media accounts to share the link or URL to your video. You can find a link by clicking on the "Share" link on the video itself. Post the link on Facebook, Twitter, Tumblr, and anywhere else you can.

If you want even more advanced YouTube tips, keep an eye out on my social media streams for a special online course I am planning to create. It will demystify some of the techniques I have learned and am actively using.

Instagram

I was active on YouTube for close to four years before I tried Instagram, and I wish I would have tried it sooner! Instagram is a great place to show off your recent mail days and tell the world about your successes. Signing up for an Instagram account is easy via Facebook or through the

Instagram website itself. One thing to keep in mind about Instagram is that it is for photos and very short videos only. When you add someone to your subscription list, that person's photostream appears in your home feed when you scroll down the page or on your phone. You can then comment and "favorite" photos.

I get more engagement on Instagram than any other social media service. One of the reasons is because I actively search out and add people who may be interested in my videos. Notifications are sent to users when others "follow" them. So, if they see you share the same type of things they do, they are more likely to follow you in turn. In addition, if you find a popular person on Instagram, you can see a list of all the people who follow them as well, and add them to the list of people you are following. This is a great way to grow your subscriber base.

ttmautograph [Follow]

TTM Autograph TTM Troy from Mike the Fan Boy and YouTube!
⬧ Youtube:troyarutter ⬧ Facebook:ttmftw.autographs www.ttmautograph.com

386 posts   **1,040** followers   **1,813** following

My main Instagram page - notice the lonely link at the top. (Troy Rutter)

You are only allowed to put a link in your profile, so linking to your YouTube videos can be a little tough. I suggest linking to your main website or your YouTube channel itself in your main profile. Then, when you add a new video to YouTube, add a thumbnail of the video to your Instagram stream and say, "New video up - link in profile" to help people find the video. Some users even do special 15-second teasers for their videos that they upload directly to Instagram. As with any social media platform, you can start small and work your way to more advanced techniques.

A couple of tips for the novice Instagram user. First, if you post a TTM success, use hashtags such as #ttm or #ttmsuccess. These will help other people find your photos. Second, when posting your photos, clearly state if they are for trade or for sale - or not. For instance, "Not FT/FS" means "Not for trade or for sale." If you don't tell people this important information, they will ask over and over. Finally, be as clear about where you sent your items (if doing TTMs) as possible. For instance, I always give a description along the lines of, "Bruce Bochy, received 2/23/2016 in 18 days via St Louis stadium. Not FS/FT. #ttm #ttmsuccess." This has all the important information. If you don't include the basic information, chances are good that someone is going to call you on it.

A final note is to pay attention to notifications on Instagram. When I first started, I had 10 direct messages in my "inbox" that I had no idea were even there. Your direct messages can be found by clicking a little icon in the upper right hand side of the app that looks like a box. If it has a red mark inside of it, you have a direct message waiting.

Facebook

When people talk about social media, many people first think of Facebook, and rightfully so. With its millions of users and mobile apps, Facebook is a popular place to connect with friends, family, and strangers via groups and pages. Choosing to create a Facebook presence for your autograph collection is a popular choice, but you have some options to consider. You can either choose to share your photos on your personal Facebook profile, create a Facebook group, or create a Facebook page.

The easiest of these alternatives is to simply post your autographs on your personal Facebook account. You can create a separate photo album and upload your autographs there. You can even create multiple albums for different types of autographs. By using your security preferences, you can set your photos as viewable by your Friends, Friends of Friends, or even make them Public. While sharing your autographs on your personal page is one of the easiest options, it makes it a little more difficult to share your photos with the larger collecting community.

My Facebook page at *facebook.com/ttmftw.autographs* (Troy Rutter)

Whether you create a Facebook page or group is up to your preference. The intricacies of differences between the two are more than I can go through in this book. In general, if you want to be the only one adding photos and news, you should create a Facebook page. If, on the other hand, you want to allow any member of to add photos to your photo galleries, you want to create a group. You can search the internet for "Facebook group vs. page" to find some great discussions on whether a page or a group is right for you. Personally, I prefer Facebook pages because I want to have my posts be the main content of the page. This gives me the ability to upload my photos and post news and have them featured prominently on the page. Posts from others will be displayed as "visitor posts" in the sidebar. Again, pick the option that is right for you.

You will need to create a separate profile image and a cover image or banner for the top of the page. Facebook will walk you through each of the different steps needed to make your new page or group public. You can name it anything you want. Some people use their real name, others do not. I named my page "Through the Mail Autograph Collecting - TTM FTW." The URL is simply "ttmftw.autographs." You have to get 25 Facebook likes in order to get your own short URL on Facebook.

Once my Facebook page was configured and growing, I started visiting other pages and liking them as my page. To do this, you simply search for another autograph page, then hover over the other page's like button. There you will see an option to "Like as your page." This will also send that page a notification that your page has "liked" their page. Hopefully they will like yours back! Once you have your page going, you will want to post photos, videos, and information regularly to keep your members entertained.

A quick note about posting videos on Facebook. For a long time I would simply post a link to my YouTube video on my Facebook page. It played and looked fine. The problem was, only a small percentage of people actually saw the video. This is because Facebook likes it when you use Facebook tools to share content. If I upload a video directly to Facebook, it reaches more of the people who like your page. One harsh reality of Facebook is that only a small percentage of the people who like your page are going to see what you post. This is so Facebook can charge you money to "boost" a post to reach more of those who like your page.

There really isn't anything you can do about it except try and play by their rules. So, upload directly to your Facebook page or group whenever you can to get the most views from your fans.

Tumblr

Tumblr is a "microblog." Posts on Tumblr tend to be shorter than normal blogs and focus a lot on photos, which is great for autographs. By posting your photos to Tumblr, other people can both like (in the form of a heart) and reblog your photo. When someone reblogs your post, it appears on their Tumblr page with a link back to yours. Over the years, I have been 50/50 on whether Tumblr is worth the time, but I currently do not use Tumblr to share my autographed photos. It is worth a try if you have time, though

Twitter

Of all the social networks featured in this chapter, Twitter is probably the least effective for sharing your autograph collection. Gaining followers on Twitter is tough, and much of the demographic you want are not the major users of the system. Over the past several years, usage on Twitter appears to have decreased significantly. The way I currently use Twitter is to tweet out the URL of my latest video to anybody who may pick up on one of my tweet's hashtags and might possibly click over to watch the video. It definitely is not on my short list of "must use" social networks for the hobby.

Snap Chat

I personally have not investigated using Snapchat to share my collection very much. If Snapchat has worked for you in sharing your autographs, please drop me an email and let me know!

Your Own Web Site

Setting up your own website is a great way to share your collection in a centralized place. In the web world, we call this your "hub." In addition to posting photos, you can link out to your other social media channels from your website, and even share your Facebook posts. Setting up your own website is not for the faint of heart, however. The easiest way to get started with your own website is to use a free service such as wordpress.com, which comes with some ready-made themes you can use.

While *wordpress.com* is good for the beginner, eventually you may want to pay for your own internet web server. There are several good companies that will allow you to do so. Whether you go with a big, national company or a small, local firm, most provide the basic Internet services to host your website for a small fee. Unless you are getting thousands of visits to your website a day, there really isn't a need to pay more than $15-$20 a month for web hosting. Some of the best I have worked with are *linode.com, hostgator.com*, and *bluehost.com*. You can find links to information on all of these in the Resources section at *ttmautograph.com*

As your website grows, you may want to get your own custom domain name so your website can be travisttms.com or something similar. Prices for a custom domain name are in addition to anything you also pay for a website.

Building Community

Building a community on social media is one of the hardest things we do as collectors. We want to tell the world about our latest successes and share in our disappointment when a TTM comes in RTS, but many people find it boring just to be told about someone else's successes. People want to feel like a part of your community and share the excitement of opening that return. They want to comment on your videos and see you commenting on theirs. One of the hardest things is finding enough time to further your own collection while also finding time to be a friend and comment on other people's videos. But making the time is definitely worth it.

On YouTube, especially, there is a way to subscribe to videos. This means that whenever someone posts a new video, the subscriber is either notified via an email or it shows up as a new video on their YouTube home page. When you subscribe to someone's channel for the first time, that person also receives a notification that someone new has subscribed. Most of the time, that person will then click on your name and check out your channel. And then you may get a reciprocal subscription. How great is that?

Comments, which can be long or short, are valued about the same as likes - everybody loves to get them. It is a good idea to comment on other people's videos that are similar to yours. Not only does it give the person reassurance their videos are being watched, but having your comment on a popular video can help create new subscribers for you as well. When someone sees your comment, they can click to your channel and subscribe to you too.

Comments should, however, have some thought behind them and be "real." I have seen people comment on videos where it was clear they hadn't watched the entire video. They post comments such as "Great vid!" when there is nothing but RTS's in the video. Whenever I comment on a video, I make sure I watch the entire thing. This helps the person who posted the video too, because according to some experts, how long people watch a video is key to YouTube featuring the video for other people to find.

When you watch a video you can also do a "thumbs up" or "thumbs down" to indicate whether you liked or didn't like a video. Even if the video quality is bad, or I can't hear anything, I never give a video a thumbs down. I may not give it a thumbs up, but giving a thumbs down should be a rarity. As a creator, it takes the wind out of your sails when you spend a lot of time creating a video only to get a bunch of "dislikes."

As much as you will hate it to happen, you will get negative comments and "dislikes" as your channel grows. It is part of creating something for others to see. People might be hateful and jealous, or may have their own personal issues. Dealing with negative comments and dislikes is something that comes with the territory. Even though every dislike "hurts," you have to learn to be numb to them and realize they probably do not dislike you, they just didn't find your particular video interesting. Occasionally people will post things in comments just to upset you, especially if you react to them. This is known as trolling, and is normal and to be expected.

I have attended several social media conferences and have read dozens of books, and each one offers differing advice as far as comments. Some say to be active in your community in the comments section, and some say to never read your comments. Personally, I prefer to be active in the comments. If someone comments on a video, I will reply "Thank you" or "Glad you liked it!" and acknowledge those who took the time to respond. If it is a negative comment, I will rarely delete the comment, even though it is easy to do so. Instead, I will just ignore the comment and try to forget about it. Oftentimes other people in your community will rally to your defense. If it gets out of control, you may have to step in to diffuse the situation. But, in general, acknowledge those making positive comments and ignore those who don't.

Contests

Contests are a way some collectors encourage community and increase their subscription numbers. There are a wide variety of contests you can do to help boost your numbers. "Sub Contests" on YouTube are particularly popular. In these contests, subscribers are encouraged to share your videos, or upload videos to their own channels mentioning your channel, receiving a point, or entry into your contest as a result. At the end of the time period, you can put all of the names and entries into a random generator such as random.org and pick out several winners who will receive prizes such as autographs, stamps, etc.

One contest I hosted recently was called Project Hit the Deck. A group of TTM collectors sent out regular playing cards to various celebrities related to the card they sent (i.e.: 9 of Clubs to someone who starred on *Deep Space 9*). Contestants received one point for every TTM they received over the run of the contest, with the winner receiving 2 rolls of 100 stamps. It was fun to see people uploading videos when they received a success in the mail and made a new video. My channel and contest were mentioned in their video as well, so it was great promotion. Think outside the box and you can probably come up with a contest your community will love.

Care Packages and Just Becauses

Care packages are another way to show your subscribers and fellow collectors you appreciate them watching your videos and being a part of your community. Care packages, or "just becauses," are gifts collectors send each other containing just about anything: unopened card packs, sharpies, stamps, top loaders, sleeves, maybe even just a short note. Since I hardly ever ask for two of the same item from a celebrity, I personally don't have many things that I can send, so I went to a website called mysharpies.com and made some custom blue sharpies to send with a simple note from time to time, thanking people for their friendship and for being part of the community. The trick with just becauses is that you have to ask people for their address, which some won't be eager to give out. Just becauses tend to increase around the holidays as people have gifting more on their minds.

Privacy

Your privacy is important. Some collectors, even though they want to share their items, don't want people to know their real name or know what they look like. That is perfectly fine. Throughout my entire Internet "career," I have always gone by my real name. This is my personal preference. Many, especially kids, create screen names that reflect what they collect. You may prefer to be known as "TTM Hunter AZ" or "card king phoenix" - the choice is completely up to you. One important thing, especially for kids, is to never give anybody your phone number or your address unless you ask your parents. It can be tempting for kids to get packages in the mail from other collectors, but if you ever hear about people asking for a child's address, be concerned and investigate immediately.

I personally chose to get a PO Box for all of my TTM collecting. The one I rent is the smallest one they have, so I get regular cards TTM without trouble. Any oversized items are held at the desk where I can pick them up. I use this address on my website and other places. This allows me to keep my personal address private. For younger collectors, or those saving money, this may not be feasible, but it is definitely an option.

Whether or not you show your face, or even use your voice, in your videos is completely up to you. There are some collectors who only show the autographs in their videos and have music playing, or even just silence as they display their recent returns. Nobody thinks less of those who value their privacy. It should also go without saying that kids need to get their parents' permission before they create any social media accounts or appear in any video. Be safe!

Sharing your collection with other like-minded collectors can be a lot of fun - and a lot of work. While I tried to touch on several different ways you can showcase your collection with other collectors, it can be a bit overwhelming if you start all of them at once. If I had to pick an order, I would suggest creating an Instagram account first, then a YouTube account, then a Facebook page, and then slowly go onto the other social media networks if you have time. Instagram is a huge heavy hitter in the autograph and card communities right now. It also has the least barriers to get started - just take a photo of your cards! Above all, have fun and make some friends. We are nice, really!

CHAPTER 13

SELLING YOUR COLLECTION

It is safe to say that the majority of TTMers and those who collect IP do so for the fun of building their own collections, but there are times when it may be desirable or necessary to consider selling items in your collection. When looking to sell your autographs, the same major websites mentioned in Chapter 10 for buying autographs also apply to selling.

When choosing which autographs to sell, I would go with items that are not personalized. While you might be able to find another fan with your first name interested in an autograph, more than likely it will be the non personalized ones that will sell.

One important thing to note, as of January 1 there is a new law in

California that will require a COA for any sold autograph over $5. You can google for "Assembly Bill 1570" for more information. Since the law is fairly new as of October 2016, there is still a lot open to interpretation.

Check Out My Cards
comc.com

COMC is a very popular website for buying and selling certified autographs as well as rare or high-end cards. They only accept autographed cards that have been slabbed and authenticated by any of the third-party-authenticators or certified cards from the major baseball card manufacturers. They do not accept TTM autographs that have not been slabbed.

Sending to COMC is a long process if you choose normal processing. Basically, after you register on their site, you create a submission request approximating the number of cards you are sending in. You then package and mail your cards, and in 4-8 weeks (for standard processing) your cards will proceed to the next step. The cost for a processing cards in the slowest amount of time is 25 cents per card, which will be deducted from your account. When starting up an account, obviously there will not be a balance to deduct from, so you will have a negative balance that builds until you begin selling your cards.

Once your cards have arrived and have begun processing, COMC scans the front and the back and adds them to your inventory. There, you can review their selected price and also the price range other sellers are offering the same card for. You set your price and add in the processing fee, and then the card is for sale. You can view my personal COMC page at *comc.com/Users/ttmautographs*.

Once cards start selling, you will be able to exchange your account balance for other cards on COMC, or withdrawal as cash for an additional fee. Because of the fee for withdrawal, many sellers on COMC use their funds to buy other cards they are looking for, and may even "flip" cards, buying for one price and then selling for a higher price.

eBay
eBay.com

eBay is the standard for selling cards - both signed and unsigned. You can find practically and card on eBay. Selling on eBay is a process that is constantly evolving if you want to keep up on the latest tips and tricks.

While running an eBay store is too lengthy to go into here, the basics are registering for an account, and then listing your autograph for sale. You will need to scan your card (some scan the front and back) and then list it on their site. You will then be charged a listing fee and a final value fee at the conclusion of the auction.

When listing your item, be sure to note as much as you can about the card or photo in the description. You will also want to clearly point out the shipping and refund rules for your auction. If you do not want to ship internationally, be sure to note that in the description and set the auction to only accept items from your own country.

If you are selling a lot of items, there are third-party website that will help ease the hassle of listing and managing items. One I currently use is Auctiva. It allows me to create my eBay listing offline, including photos and then list them all at once so they will all end at the same time. As a buyer, there is nothing more frustrating than a seller having similar auctions that span several days and then end at odd times of the night. I recommend listing items in one batch on a Saturday afternoon so they will all end in exactly one week and people can be at home battling against other bidders.

In preparation for this book, I listed several hundred autographs on eBay to help pay for the cover design. In addition to the cover, I also purchased a 4x6 label printer that will print postage I can affix to my 4x6 #000 padded envelopes. It saves time since I do not have to go to the post office. I also purchased a small postage scale, but you can find weights of cards in Appendix E in this book to find approximate weights of several trading cards when mailing.

Once the auction has completed and you have sent your items to the winning bidder, be sure to leave them feedback, especially if there weren't any difficulties. In the case of a complaint, it is best to ask them to return the item (at their expense) and refund the amount of the original auction bid.

Unless you have an extensive collection or some rare items, making a lot of money online through the sale of your TTMs is not a very likely scenario. However, it can bring in an influx of money in a pinch. Just don't expect to sell everything right away, most players who sign TTM are not in high demand and thus are lower priced.

CHAPTER 14

THE FUTURE OF AUTOGRAPH COLLECTING

Over the past few years, there has been a lot of talk about selfies becoming the "new" autograph, but the traditional hobby of autograph collecting continues to thrive. As the hobby evolves, new ways of collecting autographs will present themselves, but the tried-and-true method of getting a real signed photo or card isn't going anywhere.

The digital autograph appeared on the scene around 2013-2014. Professional players would sign an iPad with a stylus, personalizing it to a fan, and then send it via email. Several companies sprouted up to seize on this new business opportunity.

It went nowhere.

One of the more interesting trends I have seen lately is a combination of the "digital autograph" and the selfie. Everybody knows what a selfie is - a photo of yourself and possibly others, in this case with a celebrity, taken with your cell phone camera. The selfie autograph involves taking a selfie with a celebrity then having the celebrity "sign" the photo using their finger or stylus on your phone. This way, you have the selfie, but you also have a digital signature. It is an interesting new trend and impossible to sell on eBay, so celebrities may embrace it. However, I don't think it will ever take the place of something tangible like a card or a photograph.

The key is to be adaptive to change. People who loved the old gold-paint pens may have shunned the newer sharpies at first, but as they improved, the globby paint pens were replaced. In order to change and adapt, you need to be tuned into your community and always be looking for new ways to collect. Just as there are new celebrities to write to every day, there are always new collectors and new ideas entering the hobby as well.

In the end, collect autographs your way. Have fun with the hobby on your own terms. Don't compare your YouTube subscriber count or the number of autographs in your collection to other people - just have fun with it. After all, that's why we are all here.

Best wishes on your autograph endeavors, and may every day be a giant mail day!

Troy Rutter

APPENDIX A: NFL FOOTBALL ADDRESSES

Arizona Cardinals
One Cardinals Drive
Glendale, AZ 85305

Atlanta Falcons
One Georgia Dome Drive, N.W.
Atlanta, Georgia 30313

Baltimore Ravens
1101 Russell Street
Baltimore, Maryland 21230

Buffalo Bills
One Bills Drive
Orchard Park, New York 14127

Carolina Panthers
800 South Mint Street Charlotte
North Carolina 28202

Chicago Bears
Soldier Field
Chicago, Illinois 60605

Cincinnati Bengals
One Paul Brown Stadium
Cincinnati, Ohio 45202

Cleveland Browns
1085 West Third Street
Cleveland, Ohio 44114

Dallas Cowboys
1 AT&T Way
Arlington, TX 76011

Denver Broncos
1701 Bryant Street
Denver, Colorado 80204

Detroit Lions
2000 Brush Street
Detroit, Michigan 48226

Green Bay Packers
1265 Lombardi Avenue
Green Bay, Wisconsin 54307

Houston Texans
One Reliant Park
Houston, Texas 77054

Indianapolis Colts
500 South Capitol Ave
Indianapolis, IN 46225

Jacksonville Jaguars
1 Stadium Pl
Jacksonville, FL 32202

Kansas City Chiefs
1 Arrowhead Drive
Kansas City, Missouri 64129

Los Angeles Rams
911 S Figueroa St
Los Angeles, CA 90037

Miami Dolphins
2269 Dan Marino Boulevard
Miami Gardens, Florida 33056

Minnesota Vikings
401 Chicago Ave
Minneapolis, MN 55415

New England Patriots
One Patriot Place
Foxborough, MA 02035

New Orleans Saints
500 Poydras Street
New Orleans, Louisiana 70112

New York Giants
One MetLife Stadium Dr.
East Rutherford, New Jersey

New York Jets
One MetLife Stadium Dr.
East Rutherford, New Jersey

Oakland Raiders
7000 Coliseum Way
Oakland, California 94621

Philadelphia Eagles
3501 South Broad Street
Philadelphia, Pennsylvania 19101

Pittsburgh Steelers
100 Art Rooney Avenue
Pittsburgh, Pennsylvania 15212

San Diego Chargers
9449 Friars Rd
San Diego, CA 92108

San Francisco 49ers
4900 Marie P DeBartolo Way
Santa Clara, California

Seattle Seahawks
800 Occidental Avenue S.
Seattle, Washington 98134-1200

Tampa Bay Buccaneers
One Buccaneer Place
Tampa, Florida 33607

Tennessee Titans
One Titans Way
Nashville, Tennessee 37213

Washington Redskins
1600 FedEx Way
Landover, MD 20785

APPENDIX B: MAJOR LEAGUE BASEBALL ADDRESSES

Regular Season Addresses

American League

Anaheim Angels
2000 Gene Autry Way
Anaheim, CA 92806

Baltimore Orioles
333 West Camden Street
Baltimore, MD 21201

Boston Red Sox
4 Yawkey Way
Boston, MA 02215

Chicago White Sox
333 W. 35th Street
Chicago, IL 60616

Cleveland Indians
2401 Ontario Street
Cleveland, OH 44115

Detroit Tigers
2100 Woodward Avenue
Detroit, MI 48201

Kansas City Royals
1 Royal Way
Kansas City, MO 64141

Minnesota Twins
1 Twins Way
Minneapolis, MN 55403

New York Yankees
161st Street and River Avenue
Bronx, NY 10451

Oakland Athletics
7000 Coliseum Way
Oakland, CA 94621

Seattle Mariners
P. O. Box 4100
Seattle, WA 98104

Tampa Bay Devil Rays
One Tropicana Drive
St. Petersburg, FL 33705

Texas Rangers
1000 Ballpark Way
Arlington, TX 76011

Toronto Blue Jays
1 Blue Jays Way, Suite 3200
Toronto, Ontario M5V 1J1
Canada

National League

Arizona Diamondbacks
401 East Jefferson Street
Phoenix, AZ 82001

Los Angeles Dodgers
1000 Elysian Park Avenue
Los Angeles, CA 90012

Atlanta Braves
755 Hank Aaron Drive
Atlanta, GA 30315

Milwaukee Brewers
1 Brewers Way
Milwaukee, WI 53214

Chicago Cubs
1060 West Addison Street
Chicago, IL 60613

New York Mets
123-01 Roosevelt Avenue
Flushing, NY 11368

Cincinnati Reds
100 Main Street
Cincinnati, OH 45202

Philadelphia Phillies
One Citizens Bank Way
Philadelphia, PA 19148

Colorado Rockies
2001 Blake Street
Denver, CO 80205

Pittsburgh Pirates
115 Federal Street
Pittsburgh, PA 15212

Florida Marlins
2269 Dan Marino Boulevard
Miami, FL 33056

St. Louis Cardinals
250 Stadium Plaza
St. Louis, MO 63102

Houston Astros
501 Crawford Street
Houston, TX 77702

San Francisco Giants
24 Willie Mays Plaza
San Francisco, CA 94107

Washington Nationals
2400 East Capitol Street S.E.
Washington, DC 20003

Spring Training Addresses

Grapefruit League

Atlanta Braves
700 S. Victory Lane
Lake Buena Vista, FL FL 32830

Baltimore Orioles
2700 12th Street
Sarasota, FL 34237-3000

Boston Red Sox
11581 Daniels Parkway
Fort Myers, FL 33913

Detroit Tigers
2301 Lakeland Hills Blvd
Lakeland, FL 33805-5012

Houston Astros
631 Heritage Park Way
Kissimmee, FL, 34744-6110

Miami Marlins
4751 Main Street
Jupiter, FL, 33458-5203

Minnesota Twins
14100 Six Mile Cypress Parkway
Fort Myers, FL, 33912-4314

New York Mets
525 NW Peacock Blvd
Port St. Lucie, FL, 34986-2210

New York Yankees
1 Steinbrenner Drive
Tampa, FL, 33614-7064

Philadelphia Phillies
601 Old Coachman Road,
Clearwater, FL, 33765-2321

Pittsburgh Pirates
1611 Ninth Street West
Bradenton, FL, 34205-7223

St. Louis Cardinals
4751 Main Street
Jupiter, FL 33458-5203

Tampa Bay Rays
2300 El Jobean Road
Port Charlotte, FL, 33948-1120

Washington Nationals
5800 Stadium Parkway, Ste 101
Viera, FL, 32940-8013

Toronto Blue Jays
373 Douglas Avenue
Dunedin, FL, 34698-7913

Cactus League

Arizona Diamondbacks
7555 N. Pima Road
Scottsdale, AZ 85258-4013

Kansas City Royals
15960 North Bullard
Surprise, AZ, 85374

Chicago Cubs
2330 W. Rio Salado Parkway
Mesa, AZ 85201

Los Angeles Angels
2200 West Alameda Drive
Tempe, AZ, 85282-3197

Chicago White Sox
10710 West Camelback Road,
Phoenix, AZ 85037-5072

Los Angeles Dodgers
10710 W. Camelback Road
Phoenix, AZ 85037

Cincinnati Reds
1933 S. Ballpark Way
Goodyear, AZ 85338

Milwaukee Brewers
3600 N. 51st Avenue
Phoenix, AZ, 85031-3005

Cleveland Indians
1933 S. Ballpark Way
Goodyear, AZ 85338

Oakland Athletics
1235 N. Center Street
Mesa, AZ, 85201

Colorado Rockies
7555 N. Pima Road
Scottsdale, AZ 85258

San Diego Padres
16101 N. 83rd Ave
Peoria, AZ 85382-5811

San Francisco Giants
7408 East Osborn Road
Scottsdale, AZ, 85251-6424

Seattle Mariners
16101 N. 83rd Avenue
Peoria, AZ, 85382

Texas Rangers
15850 North Bullard Avenue
Surprise, AZ, 85374

APPENDIX C: AAA BASEBALL ADDRESSES

International League

Buffalo Bisons
One James D. Griffin Plaza
Buffalo NY 14203

Charlotte Knights
324 South Mint Street
Charlotte NC 28202

Columbus Clippers
330 Huntington Park Lane
Columbus OH 43215

Durham Bulls
PO Box 507
Durham NC 27702

Gwinnett Braves
PO Box 490310
Lawrenceville GA 30049

Indianapolis Indians
501 West Maryland Street
Indianapolis IN 46225

Lehigh Valley IronPigs
1050 IronPigs Way
Allentown PA 18109

Louisville Bats
401 East Main Street
Louisville KY 40202

Norfolk Tides
150 Park Avenue
Norfolk VA 23510

Pawtucket Red Sox
PO Box 2365
Pawtucket RI 02861

Rochester Red Wings
One Morrie Silver Way
Rochester NY 14608Scranton/

Wilkes-Barre RailRiders
235 Montage Mountain Road
Moosic PA 18507

Syracuse Chiefs
One Tex Simone Drive
Syracuse NY 13208

Toledo Mud Hens
406 Washington Street
Toledo OH 43604

Pacific Coast League

Albuquerque Isotopes
1601 Avenida Cesar Chavez SE -
Second Floor
Albuquerque NM 87106

Nashville Sounds
534 Chestnut Street
Nashville TN 37203

Colorado Springs Sky Sox
4385 Tutt Boulevard
Colorado Springs CO 80922

New Orleans Zephyrs
6000 Airline Drive
Metairie LA 70003

El Paso Chihuahuas
123 West Mills - Suite 300
El Paso TX 79901

Oklahoma City RedHawks
Two South Mickey Mantle Drive
Oklahoma City OK 73104

Fresno Grizzlies
1800 Tulare Street
Fresno CA 93721

Omaha Storm Chasers
12356 Ballpark Way
Papillion NE 68046

Iowa Cubs
One Line Drive
Des Moines IA 50309

Reno Aces
250 Evans Avenue
Reno NV 89501

Las Vegas 51s
850 Las Vegas Boulevard North
Las Vegas NV 89101

Round Rock Express
3400 East Palm Valley Boulevard
Round Rock TX 78665

Memphis Redbirds
175 Toyota Plaza, Suite 300
Memphis TN 38103

Sacramento River Cats
400 Ballpark Drive
West Sacramento CA 95691

Salt Lake Bees
77 West 1300 South
Salt Lake City UT 84115

Tacoma Rainiers
2502 South Tyler Street
Tacoma WA 98405

APPENDIX D: MOVIE AND TV STUDIO ADDRESSES

ABC
4151 Prospect Avenue
Los Angeles, CA 90027-4524

AMC Networks
11 Penn Plaza
New York 10001

BBC
c/o Incoming Mail
BBC Television Centre
Wood Lane
London W12 7RJ UK

CBS
7800 Beverly Boulevard
Los Angeles, CA 90036-2112

Columbia Pictures
10202 West Washington Blvd
Culver City, CA 90232-3195

Disney/Touchstone
500 South Buena Vista
Burbank, CA 91521-0001

Disney Channel
500 South Buena Vista
Burbank, CA 91521-0001

DreamWorks SKG
100 Universal City Plaza
Building 10
34th Floor
Universal City, CA 91608-1002

Food Network
75 Ninth Avenue
New York, NY 10011

FOX
10201 West Pico Boulevard
Los Angeles, CA 90064-2606

Focus Features
1540 2nd St #200
Santa Monica, CA 90401

HBO
1100 Avenue of the Americas
New York, NY 10036

Lionsgate
2700 Colorado Ave #200
Santa Monica, CA 90404

Lucasfilm LTD
5858 Lucas Valley Road
Nicasio, CA 94946-9703

Magnolia PIctures
49 West 27th Street
7th Floor, New York, NY 10001

Metro-Goldwyn-Mayer
2500 Broadway Street
Santa Monica, CA 90404-3061

Miramax Films
c/o Tribeca Film Center
375 Greenwich Street
New York, NY 10013-2338

NBC
30 Rockefeller Plaza
New York, NY 10112-0002

Netflix
100 Winchester Circle
Los Gatos, CA 95032

Paramount Pictures
5555 Melrose Avenue
Los Angeles, CA 90038-3112

Pixar Animation
1200 Park Avenue
Emeryville, California 94608

Sony Pictures Entertainment
10202 W Washington Blvd
Culver City, CA 90232

The CW
4000 Warner Blvd, Building 34R
Burbank, CA 91522-0002

Tribune Entertainment
5800 West Sunset Boulevard
Los Angeles, CA 90028-6607

Twentieth Century Fox
10201 West Pico Boulevard
Los Angeles, CA
90064-2606

Universal Pictures
100 Universal City Plaza
Universal City, CA 91608-1085

Warner Bros. Animation
15303 Ventura Boulevard
Sherman Oaks, CA 91403-3110

Warner Bros. Pictures
4000 Warner Boulevard
Burbank, CA 91522-0001

Weinstein Company
9100 Wilshire Blvd
Beverly Hills, CA 90212

APPENDIX E: INTERNATIONAL TTM POSTAGE GUIDE

Even though the methods of collecting in this book are universal, it is written from my frame of reference living in the United States. There are autograph collectors all over the world who may read this book, and while I can't go into postage rates in every single country, I can provide some information on collecting TTM autographs between other countries.

The best place to start is with standard weights of envelopes of TTM sends. On the next page, I have created a simple chart that consists of the weights of different common TTM packages. While this guide is a great starting place for figuring out postage, you should always verify the weight of your TTM letters to verify.

With the popularity of *Game of Thrones, Star Wars, Harry Potter*, and other BBS shows, sending TTMs from the US to the UK is definitely something to try for some unique autographs. Many US collectors don't normally try sending to different countries, cons celebrities in the UK may be more responsive than their US counterparts.

Common TTM Weights

The following chart lists common weights of various TTM packages. The weight is given both in ounces and grams to aid in calculating postage both on the send and SASE.

Description	Ounces	Grams
PWE, SASE, letter, 2 Cards	.50	14.1748
PWE, SASE, letter,, 3 Cards	.50	14.1748
PWE, SASE, letter,, 4 Cards	.60	17.0097
PWE, SASE, letter,, 5 Cards	.70	19.8447
PWE, SASE, letter,, 6 Cards	.70	19.8447
PWE, SASE, letter,, 7 Cards	.80	22.6796
8x10 photo, 9x12 envelope, 10x13 envelope, letter, backing board	3.30	93.5534

If you are doing a lot of TTMs that vary in weight, you may want to purchase a digital scale. These scales can be found at any office supply store and from the post office themselves. If you subscribe to a postage service such as Stamps.com, they often include a scale with their initial welcome package. If you plan on sending out a lot of similar items, using the scale at an automated kiosk will be enough.

Estimating Postage

There are two main websites to bookmark to estimate postage to and from the UK and the US and vice versa. These are: *https://postcalc.usps. com/* and *http://www.seajays.org.uk/postage/*. Be sure to use weights in ounces for the USPS site and Grams for the UK site. Don't worry about the change in weight between your send and return - the weight change is negligible, use the higher weight of the initial package for both of them.

Unless you are sending a very costly international priority mail package, in the US you will be sending everything First Class mail. You can buy specific values of First Class stamps at an automated kiosk, or you can use numerous Forever Stamps to increase the value. For instance, as of this writing a Forever stamp is worth 47 cents. Placing two on an envelope would increase the value to 94 cents. Personally, I tend to buy specific values of postage from a kiosk, but multiple stamps work as well.

A complete chart of international First Class postage can be found on the USPS Postal Explorer website at *http://pe.usps.com/text/dmm300/Notice123.htm.*

Regardless of weight, sending a normal First Class envelope and letter internationally begins at $1.15 from the United States. Sending a *Game of Thrones* card TTM to Julian Glover for instance, would cost $1.15 to send the package *to* the UK. This does *not* include the return postage on the SASE inside.

In the UK, there are two different rates of stamps: First Class and Second Class. Since mail sorting and transportation has improved over the years, many believe there is no tangible difference between the two other than price. In my experience, 2nd Class stamps are my preferred Royal Mail stamp of choice.

Using the *seajays.org.uk* website, we can input our return envelope to find out how much it will cost to send back to the U.S. In the example of the trading card sent to Julian Glover, I enter in 15 grams and then look at the shipping rate for a letter sent to World Zone 1, which includes the United States. The chart says this will cost £1.33. Since each 2nd class stamp is worth 55 pence. So, it will take 3 2nd Class stamps on the return envelope from the UK to return back to me in California.

Std World Zone 1	International Standard WZ1	Type	Standard	Signed For
	World Zone 1. International Standard aims to deliver within five working days for packages. Printed papers is for books / pamphlets only. Small Parcels is 2kg max (also maximum for Canada). Weight range at this price: **0—100g** (Large Letters **0—100g**) (Letters **11—20g**)	Letters	£1.33	£6.33
		Large Letters	£3.15	£8.35
		Parcels & Printed Papers	£4.20	£8.80

Common TTM Postage Prices Between US and UK

All of the following postage rates are estimates only and provided as an example. You should calculate exact prices at the post office, kiosk, or through one of the postage calculating websites for the current rates for your country.

When using the USPS calculations, you may need to calculate prices based on the the "Price Group" of the destination country. This chart can be found at *http://pe.usps.com/text/imm/immpg.htm*. The price group for the UK is found under Great Britain and is noted as price group 5.

Standard letters such as our favorite #10 are called Letters, and 10x13 envelopes are referred to as Large Letters as long as they are under 1 inch thick. Larger than 1 inch (25 mm) are called Parcels.

Description	US Postage	UK Postage
1 PWE, SASE, letter,1-4 Trading Cards	$1.15	£1.33 (3 2nd Class Stamps)
1 8x10 photo, 1 9x12 envelope, 1 10x13 envelope, letter, backing board	$5.10	£3.15 (6 2nd Class Stamps)

Buying Foreign Postage

I went through how to purchase Canadian stamps in the Chapter 2: Supplies. To summarize, you simply go to the Canadian Post website at *www.canadapost.ca*, buy them, and have them shipped to your address here in the US.

You can also purchase UK stamps the same way by visiting *royalmail. com.* look for stamp books of 12 second class stamps. Keep in mind that you will need 3 stamps for a regular letter, and 6 for an 8x10 return, so you may want to purchase a lot more than a booklet of 12. Since you also get charged for shipping your stamps from the UK to the US, I suggest a sheet of 100 to get your money's worth and keep you supplied for a while.

You can also buy stamps from eBay if you don't want to bother going directly to the source and waiting for an overseas shipment. You will pay extra for the convenience. For example, a book of 12 2nd Class stamps cost around $8.66 plus shipping from the Royal Post directly. On eBay, a book of 12 typically sell for around $12-$15.

FINAL THOUGHTS

I hope you have enjoyed this book as much as I have enjoyed writing it. Please reach out to me via social media and say hello and send me a link to where you post your photos on the Internet, I would love to see your collection. You can get links to all of my social media profiles at my website at *ttmautograph.com*.

Here's hoping all of us have a Giant Mail Day!

Made in the USA
San Bernardino, CA
24 October 2016